新时代商务英语专业系列教材

New Era Business English Series

总主编 / 翁凤翔　郭桂杭

Intercultural Communication in Business Context

跨文化商务交际

主　编 / 柯　威

重庆大学出版社

内 容 提 要

本书为商务领域跨文化交际素养培训教程，共12个单元，从文化总论、文化传统、价值观、身势语、人际交往等各个层面和维度分析了中西文化的差异，并通过对真实的跨文化交际案例的探讨归纳出各种场景下适当的应对方法。每个单元设计有课前热身活动(Pre-class Activity)、理论专著节选阅读(Read to Learn More)、知识拓展(Kaleidoscope)、迷你案例讨论(Mini-case Study)和课外练习(After-class Exercises)五个环节。本教材可供英语专业、商务英语专业(方向)学生使用，也可作为大学英语选修课及跨文化交际课程的教材。

图书在版编目(CIP)数据

跨文化商务交际/柯威主编.—重庆：重庆大学出版社，2017.7(2023.9重印)

商务英语专业系列教材

ISBN 978-7-5689-0200-7

Ⅰ.①跨…　Ⅱ.①柯…　Ⅲ.①商务—英语—高等学校—教材　Ⅳ.①F7

中国版本图书馆CIP数据核字(2016)第247401号

跨文化商务交际

KUAWENHUA SHANGWU JIAOJI

主编　柯　威

责任编辑：杨　琪　李　懿　　版式设计：黄俊棚

责任校对：邹　忌　　责任印制：赵　晟

*

重庆大学出版社出版发行

出版人：陈晓阳

社址：重庆市沙坪坝区大学城西路21号

邮编：401331

电话：(023) 88617190　88617185(中小学)

传真：(023) 88617186　88617166

网址：http://www.cqup.com.cn

邮箱：fxk@cqup.com.cn (营销中心)

全国新华书店经销

重庆紫石东南印务有限公司印刷

*

开本：787mm×1092mm　1/16　印张：11　字数：271千

2017年7月第1版　2023年9月第5次印刷

ISBN 978-7-5689-0200-7　定价：36.00元

总　序

商务英语作为本科专业获得教育部批准进入我国大学本科教育基本目录已经好些年了。商务英语本科专业的身份与地位获得了我国官方和外语界的认可。迄今为止，据不完全统计，有300所左右的大学开设了商务英语本科专业。各种商务英语学术活动也开始活跃。商务英语专业与英语语言文学专业、翻译专业成为我国英语教学的“三驾马车”。商务英语教学在全国已经形成较大规模，正呈良性发展态势，越来越多的大学正在积极准备申报商务英语本科专业。可以预计，将来在我国，除了研究性大学外的大部分普通本科院校的外语学院都可能开设商务英语本科专业。这是大势所趋，因为随着我国改革开放和经济全球化、世界经济一体化进程的加快，各个融入经济一体化的国家和地区急需有扎实英语功底的，熟悉国际商务基本知识的，具备国际商务领域操作技能的跨文化商务交际复合型、应用型商务英语人才。

高校商务英语专业教育首先必须有充足的合格师资；其次，需要有合适的教材。目前，虽然市面上有很多商务英语教材，但是，完整的四年商务英语本科专业教材并不多。重庆大学出版社出版的商务英语本科专业系列教材一定程度上能满足当前商务英语本科专业的教学需要。

本套系列教材能基本满足商务英语本科专业1—4年级通常开设课程的需要。商务英语专业不是商务专业而是语言专业。所以，基础年级的教材仍然是英语语言学习教材。但是，与传统的英语语言文学专业教材不同的是：商务英语专业学生所学习的英语具有显著的国际商务特色。所以，本套教材特别注重商务英语本科专业教育的特点，在基础阶段的英语技能教材中融入了商务英语元素，让学生在学习普通英语的同时，接触一些基础的商务英语语汇，通过听、说、读、写、译等技能训练，熟练掌握商务英语专业四级和八级考试词汇，熟悉基础的商务英语篇章，了解国际商务常识。

根据我国《高等学校商务英语本科专业教学质量国家标准》（以下简称《标准》），本套教材不仅包含一、二年级的基础教材，还包含高年级的继续夯实商务英语语言知识的教材，如《高级商务英语教程》1—3册等。此外，还包括英语语言文学专业学生所没有的突出商务英语本科专业特色的国际商务知识类教材，如《国际商务概论》《国际贸易实务》《国际贸易法》《市场营销》等。本套教材的总主编都是教育部商务英语专业教学协作组成员，参与了该《标准》的起草与制定，熟悉《标准》的要求，这为本套教材的质量提供了基本保障。此外，参与编写本套教材的主编及编者都是多年从事商务英语教学与研究的有经验的教师，因而，在教材的内容、体例、知识、练习以及辅助教材等方面，都充分考虑到了教材使用者的需求。教材的编写宗旨是：力求传授实用的商务英语知识和与国际商务有关领域的知识，提高学生的商务英语综合素质和跨文化商务交际能力以及思辨创新能力。

教材编写考虑到了以后推出的全国商务英语本科专业四级和专业八级的考试要求。在教材的选材、练习、词汇等方面都尽可能与商务英语本科专业四级、八级考试对接。

本套教材特别适合培养复合型、应用型的商务英语人才的商务英语本科专业的学生使用，也可作为商务英语爱好者学习商务英语的教材。教材中若存在不当和疏漏之处，敬请专家、学者及教材使用者批评指正，以便我们不断修订完善。

翁凤翔

2016年3月

前　言

在"一带一路"建设的大背景下,越来越多的中国企业将走出国门,加入对外投资合作的历史大潮中去。但是,当前中国企业国际化的程度不高,国际化的经验也不足,因此,整个劳动力市场将急需既熟练掌握一门外语,又具备跨文化交际知识和能力的国际化人才。《高等学校英语专业英语教学大纲》(以下简称《大纲》)中对外语类学生的培养目标正好契合了当前"一带一路"的国际合作的市场需要。《大纲》指出,"高等学校英语专业培养具有扎实的英语语言基础和广博的文化知识并能熟练地运用英语在外事、教育、经贸、文化、科技、军事等部门从事翻译、教学、管理、研究等工作的复合型英语人才"。为此,在课程中要设有相关专业知识课程,进一步扩大知识面,增强对文化差异的敏感性,提高综合运用英语进行交际的能力。

跨文化交流这一学科最早起源于人类学,更注重于研究不同文化间的差异。这种差异性主要体现在两个不同的层面:一方面是对不同国家、民族、文化体系的文化比较,比如东西方文化差异、中美文化差异等;另一方面,跨文化研究学者也试图通过寻找文化价值观维度或是取向以解析造成不同的文化行为和文化现象的原因,比如著名的霍夫施泰德的价值维度。而对于英语专业的学生,除了学习各国基本国情和不同的文化风俗之外,我们培养的另一个重点是跨文化交际敏感度和跨文化交际能力。因此,依据《大纲》的要求,结合商务英语的学科特点,本书编者在编写时特别注意以下几点:

1. 注意务实与实践性,商务理念贯穿全书

本书在课堂活动中设计有大量与商务活动有关的案例和问题,以培养学生在商务语境中的跨文化交际敏感度。

2. 注意培养学生思辨能力和自我学习能力

本书每个单元都有"课堂热身活动(Pre-class Activity)"和"迷你案例讨论(Mini-case Study)"两个环节,充分发挥学生的能动性、创造性,培养学生分析问题、解决问题的自主学习能力,引导学生在主动积极的思维活动中获取知识、掌握学习方法。

3. 博采众家,拓宽学生的理论知识视角

本书编者从众多经典跨文化理论专著中选取更适合本科生阅读的章节,使学生有更多的机会学习、比较本学科的研究成果。

4. 注意巩固英语语言技能,培养学生实际运用语言的能力

本书在编写之初即设立了学与练同等重要的理念,因此,每章后都配有相关的语言练习。

《跨文化商务交际》一书共编有12个单元,可满足一个学期36个学时的教学需要。每个单元设计有课前热身活动(Pre-class Activity)、理论专著节选阅读(Read to Learn More)、知识拓展(Kaleidoscope)、迷你案例讨论(Mini-case Study)和课外练习(After-class Exercises)五个环节。

编　者

2017年2月

Contents

UNIT 1 Intercultural Communication in a Globalization Context

Pre-class Activity

Grouping World Cultures

We are living in one world, but an invisible line divides the world into different countries. Some countries are like brothers and sisters, working together in all fields of international business, while some confront to each other to a deadly end. In this process, culture plays a very important role in identifying which camp you are in. Find a world map. Mark the countries you think share the same or similar cultural background and give your reasons why you group them in that way.

Read to Learn More

Text

Intercultural Communication in the Context of Globalization

By Liza Shokhina, Anton Nishchev

"*Globalization is not the only thing influencing events in the world today, but to the extent that there is a North Star and a worldwide shaping force, it is this system.*"

—Tomas Friedman

Intercultural communication between peoples is an integral attribute of the human society development. Not a single country, even the one considered most powerful in political and economic aspect, can meet cultural and aesthetic requests and needs of the humankind without applying to the world cultural heritage, spiritual heritage of other countries and peoples. The modern world is developing towards globalization. In this regard, the issues about the role and the place of international communication become an integral part of life both for the humankind in general, as well as for the individual.

Before getting deeper into these issues, we need to understand the way students perceive the term "globalization". This term is perceived in a number of ways: "the unity of capital", "disappearing of borders between nations and increasing the international division of labor", "the similarity of values among different cultures", "everybody and everything together". As it can be noticed from the results of our survey, which we held in our academic group recently, the majority of students find globalization as the unity in economic, political and cultural aspects. Taking this into consideration, we can conclude that international communication plays a great role in the process of globalization.

And what is intercultural communication? "In its most general sense international communication occurs when a member of one culture produces a message for consumption by a member of another culture. More precisely, international communication is communication between people whose cultural perceptions and symbol systems are distinct enough to alter the communication event". In spite of the fact that this phenomenon is being researched by scholars from the whole world for many years, it still remains timely and causes controversies and discussions. Under the circumstances we would like to answer the list of questions: what is the role of intercultural communication in the context of globalization? How will the process of globalization influence the humankind? Do we take into account cultural differences while we are joining the process of globalization, or do we globalize only for the sake of globalizing?

The first aspect of our attention is that societies and communities have no choice of either to participate in the process of globalization or not, but the character of their participation is shaped by specific social, cultural, economic and political conditions. This complex multi-level process of mediation between the global and local issues, being an inherent character of communication, promises to change not only the context, but likely the nature of intercultural communication. Thus, the question about the place of intercultural communication is ambiguous.

On the one hand, due to intercultural communication, nations can engage in a dialog and find understanding during the process of searching and making decisions in crisis, critical, nonstandard situations. Not to make unsubstantiated statements, the recent summit G-20 in London can be given. Countries with diametrically opposite points of view on the economic crisis's roots managed to find consensus and start working out a common approach to the solution of worldwide problems. Another example to illustrate the same point is the Cuban missile crisis in 1962, when the whole world was standing on the brink of a nuclear war. The two leaders from a communist and a capitalist great powers made an agreement, which prevented humankind from treat of death.

On the other hand, there are a lot of grievous examples when countries were unable to find understanding and to solve urgent problems and conflicts. This can be referred to as in the situations between Serbia and Kosovo, South Ossetia and Georgia, Moldova and Transnistria, Palestine and Israel. In each of these conflicts, opposing forces suppose they held the only right and appropriate opinions regarding the issues, and they did not want to compromise, and therefore civilians suffered.

In retrospect to the previous experience of the world history, we can ask a question: "Is the idea of a 'uniform' humankind feasible?" Can you imagine the situation when everyone has similar culture with similar values and similar beliefs? Maybe, in such world community, there will be no misunderstanding and obstacles in the process of communication. This would also mean the destruction of cultural diversity as a result of globalization. In such a case, the seemingly positive side of cultural destruction can be presented in the following way:

Destruction of cultural diversity →destruction of communication obstacles →easiness to find understanding and to solve problems.

It seems to also provide a great impulse to the development of society in economic and political aspects. But, if we scrutinize this problem, we can find a big amount of disadvantages connected with this outcome. Our cultural heritage would turn into dust because "culture is communication; communication is culture". Moreover, due to the fact that this process of globalization is done by the "upper" side (according to the will of the strongest) the opinion of individuals (national minorities) is not taken into consideration; therefore resistance against globalization will increase. It casts doubt on the idea of a totally globalized world. If this problem is solved by radical measures, two worlds will be able to appear: the world of supporters and the world of opponents who will never have their place in such a world.

The above given contemplation allows us to make a conclusion, that the process of globalization is everlasting. Under the circumstances, the era of globalization has at least two trends regarding its cultural aspect development. On the one hand, globalization is changing the traditional lifestyles of people. But on the other hand, some adaptation and protecting functions of each culture are generated, so the process of globalization takes an extremely controversial format. Within the bounds of intercultural communication, some common values and ideals (tolerance, equality of traditions, ethics and politics of responsibility) are being formed. However, the process of creation of commonalities within communicational interaction is not always smooth. For example, such universal values as human rights, which were accepted by some countries as basic values, turn out to be incompatible with the political and cultural customs of other countries. In order to prevent such incompatibilities, countries must find points of contact in which the principles of globalization do not contradict customs and traditions of these countries. Then, as we view it, the points of mutual contact should be found. In cases when it seems impossible to find points of mutual contact, countries should demonstrate tolerance and respect to each other. In this connection we can declare that the future of humankind depends only on us and on our actions towards each other. And understanding this is one of the many steps which mankind must take in order to prosper together in peace.

After reading activity

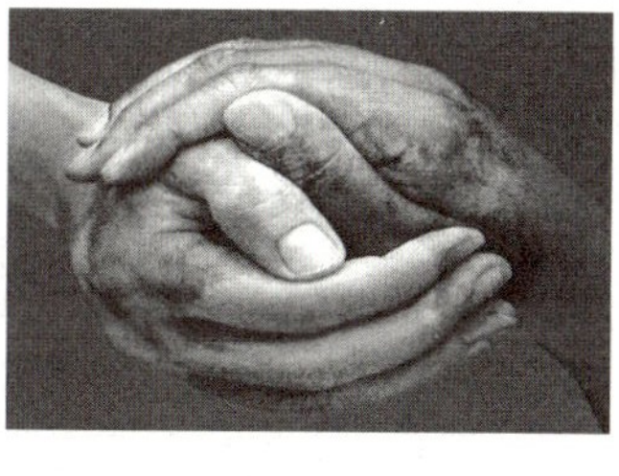

1. Name some international organizations you know or your country belongs to, and list fields in which your country can operate with other countries. Discuss difficulties or obstacles that may be

encountered in cooperation and look for the cultural factors that hinder the cooperation.

2. Model United Nations.

Work as teams to form delegations from different nations. The debate topic for the two parties is *how to face the challenges brought by refugee crisis*. The whole process should include at least three stages: debate, negotiation and resolution draft.

Kaleidoscope

The Three Major World Economic and Trade Organizations

Organization	Description
The World Trade Organization (WTO)	The World Trade Organization (WTO) is the only global international organization dealing with the rules of trade between nations. At its heart are the WTO agreements, negotiated and signed by the bulk of the world's trading nations and ratified in their parliaments. The goal is to help producers of goods and services, exporters, and importers conduct their business.
The International Monetary Fund (IMF)	The International Monetary Fund (IMF) is an organization of 188 countries, working to foster global monetary cooperation, secure financial stability, facilitate international trade, promote high employment and sustainable economic growth, and reduce poverty around the world.
The World Bank	The World Bank is a United Nations international financial institution that provides loans to developing countries for capital programs. The World Bank is a component of the World Bank Group, and a member of the United Nations Development Group.

Major Regional Economic and Trade Groups

Organization	Description
North American Free Trade Agreement (NAFTA)	On January 1, 1994, the North American Free Trade Agreement between the United States, Canada, and Mexico (NAFTA) entered into force. All remaining duties and quantitative restrictions were eliminated, as scheduled, on January 1, 2008. NAFTA created the world's largest free trade region, which now links 450 million people producing $17 trillion worth of goods and services.

Continued

Organization	Description
Association of South-Eastern Asian Nations (ASEAN)	The ASEAN Free Trade Area (AFTA) is a trade bloc agreement motioned by the Association of Southeast Asian Nations supporting local manufacturing in all ASEAN countries. The AFTA agreement was signed on 28 January 1992 in Singapore. When the AFTA agreement was originally signed, ASEAN had six members, namely, Brunei, Indonesia, Malaysia, Philippines, Singapore and Thailand. Vietnam joined it in 1995, Laos and Myanmar in 1997 and Cambodia in 1999. AFTA now comprises the ten countries of ASEAN. All the four latecomers were required to sign the AFTA agreement in order to join ASEAN, but were given longer time frames in which to meet AFTA's tariff reduction obligations.
Asia-Pacific Economic Cooperation (APEC)	Asia-Pacific Economic Cooperation (APEC) is a forum for 21 Pacific Rim member economies that seeks to promote free trade and economic cooperation throughout the Asia-Pacific region. It was established in 1989 in response to the growing interdependence of Asia-Pacific economies and the advent of regional trade blocs in other parts of the world; to fears that highly industrialized Japan (a member of G8) would come to dominate economic activity in the Asia-Pacific region; and to establish new markets for agricultural products and raw materials beyond Europe (where demand had been declining).
European Union (EU)	The European Union (EU) is a politico-economic union of 28 member states that are primarily located in Europe. The EU operates through a system of supranational independent institutions and intergovernmental negotiated decisions by the member states. Institutions of the EU include the European Commission, the Council of the European Union, the European Council, the Court of Justice of the European Union, the European Central Bank, the Court of Auditors, and the European Parliament. The European Parliament is elected every five years by EU citizens.
Group of Eight (G8)	The Group of Eight (G8) was the name of a forum for the governments of a group of eight leading industrialised countries that was originally formed by six leading industrialised countries and subsequently extended with two additional members. Russia, which was invited to join as the last member, was excluded from the forum by the other members on March 24, 2014, as a result of its involvement in the 2014 Crimea crisis in Ukraine. Thus the group now comprises seven nations and will continue to meet as the G7 group of nations.

Mini-case Study

Alibaba's American Dream

Described as a mix of eBay (EBAY), PayPal, Amazon.com (AMZN) and Google (GOOGL), Alibaba is the 800-pound gorilla in China's Internet economy, but it has little presence elsewhere in the world.

So what happens when Alibaba comes to the U.S.?

After the IPO, Alibaba will have billions of extra cash on hand. The company is likely to use some of those funds to shake up American commerce and Silicon Valley.

"If Alibaba buys its way into the U.S. economy, which they ought to be able to do, they may be able to become a North American brand," said Roger Kay, president of Endpoint Technologies Associates.

Alibaba's decision to list in New York came after the exchange in Hong Kong balked at the company's proposed governance structure, which would have breached rules there by allowing senior executives to nominate the majority of the board. Listing in the U.S. also offers the company an opportunity to introduce itself to American consumers.

The Chinese company has already made ripples in the U.S., shelling out hundreds of millions of dollars since the beginning of 2013 on investments in a slew of companies, including Uber-like app Lyft, social network Tango, app search engine Quixey and online shopping service ShopRunner.

Alibaba also continues to spend money on assets within China. Last week the company spent $1.22 billion to acquire an 18.5% stake in China's YoukuTudou, an online video company likened to both YouTube and Netflix.

These deals show how the Chinese company is already adroit at scooping up top talent around the world, including in Silicon Valley.

But Alibaba looks ready to move beyond just acquiring American startups and into direct competition in the U.S.

The company recently announced plans to launch 11main.com, a new e-commerce site in the U.S. that will offer high-quality products from assorted merchants.

"I'm pretty skeptical because I think there's definitely a lack of familiarity of the Alibaba brand and business," said Scott Kessler, head of technology equity research at S&P Capital IQ.

While Alibaba may be able to offer value to customers, Kessler said it will take time to "cultivate and build trust" among American consumers who are often skeptical of Chinese companies.

Alibaba also faces cultural and, more importantly, competitive challenges in the mature U.S. market.

"Whether they can compete on a truly level global playing field is an open question. As strong as Alibaba is in China, Amazon is that strong here in the U.S.," said Josh Green, founder and CEO of Panjiva, an intelligence platform for global trade professionals.

Questions for discussion

1. What is Chinese business culture?
2. What is American business culture?
3. What attitude do American customers hold to Chinese companies and products?
4. What challenges will Alibaba face in American market?
5. What values should Alibaba act on in a global business setting?

After-class Exercises

A Multipolar, Multicivilizational World

In the post-Cold War world, for the first time in history, global politics has become multipolar and multicivilizational. During most of human existence, contacts between civilizations were intermittent or nonexistent. Then, with the beginning of the modern era, about A.D. 1500, global politics assumed two dimensions. For over four hundred years, the nation states of the West—Britain, France, Spain, Austria, Prussia, Germany, the United States, and others—constituted a multipolar international system within Western civilization and interacted, competed, and fought wars with each other. At the same time, Western nations also expanded, conquered, colonized, or decisively influenced every other civilization. During the Cold War global politics became bipolar and the world was divided into three parts. A group of mostly wealthy and democratic societies, led by the United States, was engaged in a pervasive ideological, political, economic, and, at times, military competition with a group of somewhat poorer communist societies associated with and led by the Soviet Union. Much of this conflict occurred in the Third World outside these two camps, composed of countries which often were poor, lacked political stability, were recently independent, and claimed to be nonaligned. In the late 1980s the communist world collapsed, and the Cold War international system became history. In the post-Cold War world, the most important distinctions among peoples are not ideological, political, or economic. They are cultural. Peoples and nations are attempting to answer the most basic question humans can face: *Who* are we? And they are answering that question in the traditional way human beings have answered it, by reference to the things that mean most to them. People define themselves in terms of ancestry, religion, language, history, values, customs, and institutions. They identify with cultural groups: tribes, ethnic groups, religious communities, nations, and, at the broadest level, civilizations. People use politics not just to advance their interests but also to define their identity. We know who we are only when we know who we are not and often only when we know whom we are against.

Nation states remain the principal actors in world affairs. Their behavior is shaped as in the past by the pursuit of power and wealth, but it is also shaped by cultural preferences, commonalities, and differences. The most important groupings of states are no longer the three blocs of the Cold War but rather the world's seven or eight major civilizations. Non-Western societies, particularly in East Asia, are developing their economic wealth and creating the basis for enhanced military power and political influence. As their power and self-confidence increase, non-Western societies increasingly assert their own cultural values and reject those "imposed" on them by the West. The "international system of the twenty-first century," Henry Kissinger has noted, "... will contain at least six major powers—the United States, Europe, China, Japan, Russia, and probably India—as well as a multiplicity of medium-sized and smaller countries." Kissinger's six major powers belong to five very different civilizations, and in addition there are important Islamic states whose strategic locations, large populations, and/or oil resources make them influential in world affairs. In this new world, local politics is the politics of ethnicity; global politics is the politics of civilizations. The rivalry of the superpowers is replaced by the clash of civilizations.

In this new world, the most pervasive, important, and dangerous conflicts will not be between social classes, rich and poor, or other economically defined groups, but between peoples belonging to different cultural entities. Tribal wars and ethnic conflicts will occur within civilizations. Violence between states and groups from different civilizations, however, carries with it the potential for escalation as other states and groups from these civilizations rally to the support of their "kin countries". The bloody clash of clans in Somalia poses no threat of broader conflict. The bloody clash of tribes in Rwanda has consequences for Uganda, Zaire, and Burundi but not much further. The bloody clashes of civilizations in Bosnia, the Caucasus, Central Asia, or Kashmir could become bigger wars. In the Yugoslav conflicts, Russia provided diplomatic support to the Serbs, and Saudi Arabia, Turkey, Iran, and Libya provided funds and arms to the Bosnians, not for reasons of ideology or power politics or economic interest but because of cultural kinship. "Cultural conflicts," Vaclav Havel has observed, "are increasing and are more dangerous today than at any time in history," and Jacques Delors agreed that "future conflicts will be sparked by cultural factors rather than economics or ideology." And the most dangerous cultural conflicts are those along the faultlines between civilizations.

In the post-Cold War world, culture is both a divisive and a unifying force. People separated by ideology but united by culture come together, as the two Germanys. Societies united by ideology or historical circumstance but divided by civilization either come apart, as did the Soviet Union, Yugoslavia, and Bosnia, or are subjected to intense strain, as is the case with Ukraine, Nigeria, Sudan, India, Sri Lanka, and many others. Countries with cultural affinities cooperate economically and politically. International organizations based on states with cultural commonality, such as the European Union, are far more successful than those that attempt to transcend cultures. For forty-five years the Iron Curtain was the central dividing line in Europe. That line has moved several hundred miles east. It is now the line separating the peoples of Western Christianity, on the one hand, from Muslim and Orthodox peoples on the other.

The philosophical assumptions, underlying values, social relations, customs, and overall outlooks on life differ significantly among civilizations. The revitalization of religion throughout much of the world is reinforcing these cultural differences. Cultures can change, and the nature of their impact on politics and economics can vary from one period to another. Yet the major differences in political and economic development among civilizations are clearly rooted in their different cultures. East Asian economic success has its source in East Asian culture, as do the difficulties East Asian societies have had in achieving stable democratic political systems. Islamic culture explains in large part the failure of democracy to emerge in much of the Muslim world. Developments in the postcommunist societies of Eastern Europe and the former Soviet Union are shaped by their civilizational identities.

The West is and will remain for years to come the most powerful civilization. As the West attempts to assert its values and to protect its interests, non-Western societies confront a choice. Some attempt to emulate the West and to join or to "bandwagon" with the West. Other Confucian and Islamic societies attempt to expand their own economic and military power to resist and to "balance" against the West. A central axis of post-Cold War world politics is thus the interaction of Western power and culture with the power and culture of non-Western civilizations.

In sum, the post-Cold War world is a world of seven or eight major civilizations. Cultural commonalities and differences shape the interests, antagonisms, and associations of states. The most important countries in the world come overwhelmingly from different civilizations. The local conflicts most likely to escalate into broader wars are those between groups and states from different civilizations. The predominant patterns of political and economic development differ from civilization to civilization. The key issues on the international agenda involve differences among civilizations. Power is shifting from the long predominant West to non-Western civilizations. Global politics has become multipolar and multicivilizational.

(Huntington, Samuel P. 1989. *The Clash of Civilization and the Remarking of World Order*. New York: Simon & Schuster, pp. 21-29)

Questions

1. How do cultures help to give rise to the current world system?
2. Why can culture be used to explain the unbalanced development of world economic and political system? For example, "East Asian economic success has its source in East Asian culture, as do the difficulties East Asian societies have had in achieving stable democratic political systems. Islamic culture explains in large part the failure of democracy to emerge in much of the Muslim world." Explain it.

UNIT 2 Concept of Culture

Pre-class Activity

Getting to Know Your Culture

The time is set in the ancient China. A new business is going to open. Your boss has assigned you the following tasks. Work in groups to discuss how to complete these tasks:

1) An opening ceremony for the new business.
   List objects that are used in the opening ceremony and explain their usage or function.
2) The schedule of the opening day.
   Think about some activities or events that may be held on the opening day. Draw a flowchart to illustrate the procedures one needs to follow.
3) The guests.
   Suppose your boss is a successful and influential businessman in the local community. Who are you going to invite on the opening day and why do you invite them?
4) The changed or unchanged tradition.
   Comparing with the common practices of celebration of a newly-open business, discuss what have changed or not changed. And explain why?
5) How to greet guests and what should you say to the guests?
   Act it out in a situational mini-skit.

Discussion: Based on the experiences above, what is your own definition of culture?

Read to Learn More

Text

Culture as Products, Practices, Perspectives, Communities, and Persons

By Patrick R. Moran

This view of culture is understandable and relatively easy to apply, with two important exceptions. Cultural artifacts, actions, and meanings do not exist apart from the people of the culture. People—alone and with others—make and use artifacts, carry out actions, and hold meanings. To capture the active role of people in their culture, I have added two dimensions to this definition: communities and persons. The diagram below illustrates the interplay of these five dimensions.

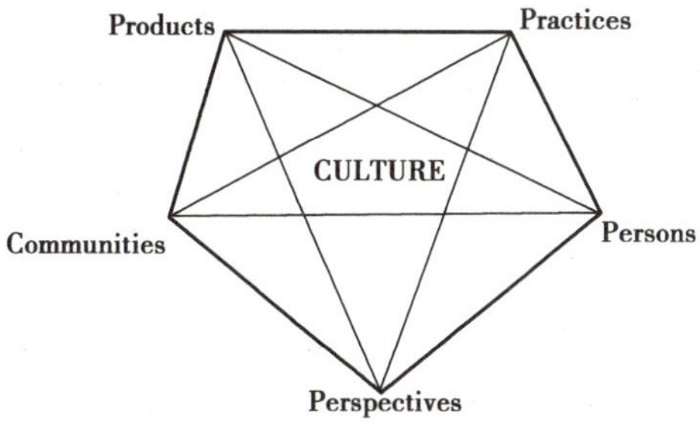

The Five Dimensions of Culture

Drawing upon these five interrelated dimensions, I define culture as follows: *Culture is the evolving way of life of a group of persons, consisting of a shared set of practices associated with a shared set of products, based upon a shared set of perspectives on the world, and set within specific social contexts.*

◆ The **evolving way of life** reflects the dynamic nature of culture—that there is a history and tradition to the products, practices, perspectives, and the communities of the culture. It also stresses that the persons of the culture are in the process of actively creating and changing products, practices, perspectives, and communities.

◆ **Products** are all artifacts produced or adopted by the members of culture, including those in the environment, such as plants and animals. Products range from tangible objects—such as tools, clothing, written documents, or buildings—to more elaborate yet still perceptible constructions such as written and spoken language, music, or complex institutions of family, education, economy, politics, and religion. Products, both the tangible and intangible, are located and organized in physical places.

◆ **Practices** comprise the full range of actions and interactions that members of the culture carry out, individually or with others. These include language and other forms of communication and self-expression as well as actions associated with social groups and use of products. These practices are both verbal and nonverbal and include interpretations of time, space, and the context of communication in social situations. Practices also involve notions of appropriateness and inappropriateness, including taboos.

◆ **Perspectives** represent the perceptions, beliefs, values, and attitudes that underlie the products and that guide persons and communities in the practices of the culture. These perspectives can be explicit but often they are implicit, outside conscious awareness. Taken as a whole, perspectives provide meaning and constitute a unique outlook or orientation toward life—a worldview.

- **Communities** consist of the specific groups of the culture in which members, through different kinds of interpersonal relationships, carry out practices in specific social and physical settings. Such groups of people range from broad, amorphous communities like nation, language, gender, race, religion, socioeconomic class, region, or generation to more narrowly defined grouping: a workplace, a neighborhood, an alumni association of a particular school, a local political party, a religious social club, a sports team, a charity organization, coworkers, or family. These communities coexist within the national culture and are in particular relationships with one another: separation, cooperation, collaboration or conflict.
- **Persons** constitute the individual members who embody the culture and its communities in unique ways. Each person is a distinct mix of its communities and experiences, and all persons take on a particular cultural identity that both links them to and separates them from other members of the culture. Culture resides both in the individual members of the culture and in the various social groups or communities that these persons form to carry out their way of life. Culture is thus both individual and collective—psychological and social.

This definition holds that there are five dimensions to all cultural phenomena. I use the term *cultural phenomenon* broadly, simply as a way of defining a cultural topic. A cultural phenomenon involves tangible forms or structures (products) that individual members of the culture (persons) use in various interactions (practices) in specific social circumstances and groups (communities) in ways that reflect their values, attitudes, and beliefs (perspectives). Cultural phenomena can therefore be identified from any of these five dimensions. By looking for the connections from one to the other four, we can develop a more profound and informed picture of a culture.

(Excerpted from Moran, Patrick R. 2002. *Teaching Culture: Perspectives in Practice*. Beijing: Foreign Language Teaching and Research Press, pp. 24-26)

After reading activity

1. Please reflect on the business-opening activities you did at the pre-class activity section and try to interpret this cultural phenomenon from different dimensions.
2. People from different cultures have different concepts on food and dining. We use different utensils to eat and set rules about the appropriate use of them. All of these etiquettes are called tabel manners. Interview your partner, find the table manners their family conduct at the dinner table and search for information on tableware and table rules from other countries, exploring the cultural values behind those practices.

Kaleidoscope

More Definitions of Culture

- By culture we mean all those historically created designs for living, explicit and implicit, rational, irrational, and non-rational, which exist at any given time as potential guides for the behavior of men."
  (Kluckhohn, C. & Kelly, W. H. 1945. "The concept of culture". In R. Linton (Ed.). *The Science of Man in the World Culture*. New York. pp. 78-105.)
- A culture is a configuration of learned behaviors and results of behavior whose component elements are shared and transmitted by the members of a particular society.
  (Linton, R. 1945. *The Cultural Background of Personality*. New York: Greenwood-Heinemann Publishing, p. 32.)
- Culture consists of patterns, explicit and implicit, of and for behavior acquired and transmitted by symbols, constituting the distinctive achievements of human groups, including their embodiments in artifacts; the essential core of culture consists of traditional (i.e. historically derived and selected) ideas and especially their attached values; culture systems may, on the one hand, be considered as products of action, and on the other as conditioning elements of further action.
  (Kroeber, A. L. & Kluckhohn, C. 1952. *Culture: A critical review of concepts and definitions*. Cambridge: Harvard University Peabody Museum of American Archeology and Ethnology Papers, p. 47.)
- Culture has been defined in a number of ways, but most simply, as the learned and shared behavior of a community of interacting human beings.
  (Useem, J. & Useem, R. 1963. "The Interfaces of a Binational Third Culture: A Study of the American Community in India". *Human Organizations*, 22(3).)
- Culture is the collective programming of the mind which distinguishes the members of one category of people from another.
  (Hofstede, G. 1984. "National cultures and corporate cultures". In L.A. Samovar & R.E. Porter (Eds.). *Communication Between Cultures*. Belmont, CA: Wadsworth, p. 51.)
- Culture is the shared knowledge and schemes created by a set of people for perceiving, interpreting, expressing, and responding to the social realities around them.

(Lederach, J. P. 1995. *Preparing for Peace: Conflict Transformation Across Cultures*. Syracuse, NY: Syracuse University Press, p. 9.)

Mini-case Study

Handle to a Culture

When I first moved to North America from Hong Kong, local friends would invite me to their homes for tea. I would watch them bring out their large teapot, throw in some tea leaves, add boiling water and let the leaves steep until the brew was very strong. When the tea got too strong, they would simply add more water and repeat the process until the leaves had no more flavour. They were surprised to learn that this is how most Chinese drink tea as well!

While most Chinese are aware of Gong Fu Cha as part of their cultural history, few actually know how it is done. The modern Gong Fu style of tea-making is essentially about controlling all the variables of tea-making with a high degree of precision and consistency. In this way it is possible to get the maximum flavour consistently from the maximum number of brews that a tea can make. It is not a ceremony as with the well known Japanese Cha No Yu tradition with all its symbolism, but a procedure of practical steps where everything involved has a functional purpose to make a tea taste as good as possible.

Gong Fu Cha is as much about escaping the pressures of life for a few moments as it is about enjoying every drop of tea. The first thing a Westerner will notice is that the teacups are very small. This approach to tea-making with such attention to detail and savouring every drop is different from western notions, but as an art that has been perfected over many hundreds of years, the result is a relaxing and enjoyable environment alone or with friends and tea that tastes better than you've ever tasted before. With many Chinese tea shops now opening and with wide access to the internet, tea knowledge, good quality tea and tea accessories are more widely available than ever before, so anyone from anywhere can learn this ancient skill with just a little practice!

Questions for discussion

1. Identify the five cultural dimensions in this story.
2. Explain how the five dimensions link to each other in this story.

After-class Exercises

Reading

What Is Culture?

The word *culture* has many different meanings. For some it refers to an appreciation of good literature, music, art, and food. For a biologist, it is likely to be a colony of bacteria or other micro-organisms growing in a nutrient medium in a laboratory Petri dish. However, for anthropologists and other behavioral scientists, culture is the full range of learned human behavior patterns. The term was first used in this way by the pioneer English Anthropologist Edward B. Tylor in his book, *Primitive Culture*, published in 1871. Tylor said that culture is "that complex whole which includes knowledge, belief, art, law, morals, custom, and any other capabilities and habits acquired by man as a member of society". Of course, it is not limited to men. Women possess and create it as well. Since Tylor's time, the concept of culture has become the central focus of anthropology.

Culture is a powerful human tool for survival, but it is a fragile phenomenon. It is constantly changing and easily lost because it exists only in our minds. Our written languages, governments, buildings, and other man-made things are merely the products of culture. They are not culture in themselves. For this reason, archaeologists can not dig up culture directly in their excavations. The broken pots and other artifacts of ancient people that they uncover are only material remains that reflect cultural patterns—they are things that were made and used through cultural knowledge and skills.

There are very likely three layers or levels of culture that are part of your learned behavior patterns and perceptions. Most obviously is the body of cultural traditions that distinguish your specific society. When people speak of Italian, Samoan, or Japanese culture, they are referring to the shared language, traditions, and beliefs that set each of these peoples apart from others. In most cases, those who share your culture do so because they acquired it as they were raised by parents and other family members who have it.

The second layer of culture that may be part of your identity is a subculture. In complex, diverse societies in which people have come from many different parts of the world, they often retain much of their original cultural traditions. As a result, they are likely to be part of an identifiable subculture in their new society. The shared cultural traits of subcultures set themselves apart from the rest of their society. Examples of easily identifiable subcultures in the United States include ethnic groups such as Vietnamese Americans, African Americans, and Mexican Americans. Members of each of these subcultures share a common identity, food tradition, dialect or language, and other cultural traits that come from their common ancestral background and experience. As the cultural differences between members of a subculture and the dominant national culture blur and eventually disappear, the subculture ceases to exist except as a group of people who claim a common ancestry. That is generally the case with German Americans and Irish Americans in the United States today. Most of them identify themselves as Americans first. They also see themselves as being part of the cultural mainstream of the nation.

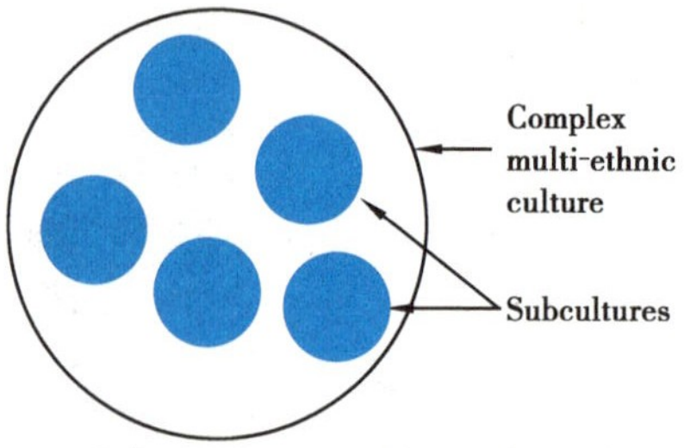

The third layer of culture consists of cultural universals. These are learned behavior patterns that are shared by all of humanity collectively. No matter where people live in the world, they share these universal traits.

While all cultures have these and possibly many other universal traits, different cultures have developed their own specific ways of carrying out or expressing them. For instance, people in deaf subcultures frequently use their hands to communicate with sign language instead of verbal language. However, sign languages have grammatical rules just as verbal ones do.

Culture and society are not the same thing. While cultures are complexes of learned behavior patterns and perceptions, societies are groups of interacting organisms. People are not the only animals that have societies. Schools of fish, flocks of birds, and hives of bees are societies. In the case of humans, however, societies are groups of people who directly or indirectly interact with each other. People in human societies also generally perceive that their society is distinct from other societies in terms of shared traditions and expectations.

While human societies and cultures are not the same thing, they are inextricably connected because culture is created and transmitted to others in a society. Cultures are not the product of lone individuals. They are the continuously evolving products of people interacting with each other. Cultural patterns such as language and politics make no sense except in terms of the interaction of people. If you were the only human on earth, there would be no need for language or government.

There is a difference of opinion in the behavioral sciences about whether or not we are the only animal that creates and uses culture. The answer to this question depends on how narrow culture is defined. If it is used broadly to refer to a complex of learned behavior patterns, then it is clear that we are not alone in creating and using culture. Many other animal species teach their young what they themselves learned in order to survive. This is especially true of the chimpanzees and other relatively intelligent apes and monkeys. Wild chimpanzee mothers typically teach their children about several hundred food and medicinal plants. Their children also have to learn about the dominance hierarchy and the social rules within their communities. As males become teenagers, they acquire hunting skills from adults. Females have to learn how to nurse and care for their babies. Chimpanzees even have to learn such basic skills as how to perform sexual intercourse. This knowledge is not hardwired into their brains at birth. They are all learned patterns of behavior just as they are for humans.

1. Human culture is ________.
   A. partly inherited genetically
   B. entirely learned
   C. limited to relatively rich societies with sophisticated technologies
   D. All of the above.
2. Which of the following statements is true of culture?
   A. Language are cultures.
   B. Archaeologists dig up culture in their excavations.
   C. Culture is a powerful human tool for survival.
   D. All of the above.
3. Who first defined culture as "that complex whole which includes knowledge, belief, art, law, morals, custom, and any other capabilities and habits acquired by man as a member of society"?
   A. E. B. Tylor. B. The author of this tutorial.
   C. Tylor Edwards. D. None of the above.
4. A ________ is a regional, social, or ethnic group that is distinguishable from other groups in a society by the fact that its members share a common identity, food tradition, dialect or language, and other cultural traits that come from their common ancestral background and experience.
   A. culture B. subculture
   C. multi-ethnic society D. None of the above.
5. Which of the following things would be cultural universals? (Think in term of the way "cultural universal" is used in this tutorial.)
   A. The language that you speak.
   B. The styles of clothes that you wear.
   C. The specific knowledge that you acquired in school.
   D. None of the above.
6. Culture is ________.
   A. the same thing as society B. limited to humans
   C. possessed only by males D. None of the above.
7. Societies are ________.
   A. groups of interacting organisms

B. only found among humans
C. created only by technologically sophisticated peoples such as those in the industrialized nations of the world
D. None of the above.

Movie Theatre

The Wedding Banquet is a 1993 film about a gay Taiwanese immigrant man who marries a mainland Chinese woman to placate his parents and get her a green card. His plan backfires when his parents arrive in the United States to plan his wedding banquet. The film was directed by Ang Lee and stars Winston Chao, May Chin, Ah Lei Gua, Sihung Lung, and Mitchell Lichtenstein.

Watch this movie and write a movie review.

UNIT 3 Conflicts of Systems

Pre-class Activity

Giving Advices to a Foreign Institution

In a global business world, the cultural systems, such as economic systems, political systems, legal systems, educational systems, marriage and family systems, and so on, have had a great impact on multicultural communication. Knowing how one country's cultural systems differ from others would enhance communication effectiveness when conducting business with companies or persons of other cultures. Here is a situation: an American educational institution wants to open a branch in China, so they come to you for advices. Your advices should be given concerning the following aspects:

- Chinese political system
- Chinese economic system
- Chinese educational system

Tell them how these systems in China differ from those in USA, and try to explain these differences from the perspective of culture.

Read to Learn More

Text

Types of Economic Systems

Scarcity is the fundamental challenge confronting all individuals and nations. We all face limitations... so we all have to make choices. We can't always get what we want. How we deal with these limitations—that is, how we prioritize and allocate our limited income, time, and resources—is the basic economic challenge that has confronted individuals and nations throughout history.

But not every nation has addressed this challenge in the same way. Societies have developed different broad economic approaches to manage their resources. Economists generally recognize four basic types of economic systems—traditional, command, market, and mixed—but they don't completely agree on the question of which system best addresses the challenge of scarcity.

A *traditional economic system* is shaped by tradition. The work that people do, the goods and services they provide, how they use and exchange resources... all tend to follow long-established patterns. These economic systems are not very dynamic—things don't change very much. Standards of living are static; individuals don't enjoy much financial or occupational mobility. But economic behaviors and relationships are predictable. You know what you are supposed to do, who you trade with, and what to expect from others.

In many traditional economies, community interests take precedence over the individual. Individuals may be expected to combine their efforts and share equally in the proceeds of their labor. In other traditional economies, some sort of private property is respected, but it is restrained by a strong set of obligations that individuals owe to their community.

Today you can find traditional economic systems at work among Australian aborigines and some isolated tribes in the Amazon jungle. In the past, they could be found everywhere—in the feudal agrarian villages of Medieval Europe, for example.

In a *command economic system* or *planned economy*, the government controls the economy. The state decides how to use and distribute resources. The government regulates prices and wages; it may even determine what sorts of work individuals do. Historically, the government has assumed varying degrees of control over the economy in socialist countries. In some, only major industries have been subjected to government management; in others, the government has exercised far more extensive control over the economy.

The classic (failed) example of a command economy was the former communist Soviet Union. The collapse of the communist bloc in the late 1980s led to the demise of many command economies around the world; Cuba continues to hold on to its planned economy even today.

In *market economies*, economic decisions are made by individuals. The unfettered interaction of individuals and companies in the marketplace determines how resources are allocated and goods are distributed. Individuals choose how to invest their personal resources—what training to pursue, what jobs to take, what goods or services to produce. And individuals decide what to consume. Within a *pure market economy* the government is entirely absent from economic affairs.

The United States in the late nineteenth century, at the height of the laissez-faire era, was about as close as we've seen to a pure market economy in modern practice.

A *mixed economic system* combines elements of the market and command economy. Many economic decisions are made in the market by individuals. But the government also plays a role in the allocation and distribution of resources.

The United States today, like most advanced nations, is a mixed economy. The eternal question for mixed economies is just what the right mix between the public and private sectors of the economy should be.

Why It Matters Today

Half of the twentieth century went down as a global battle between defenders of free markets (democratic capitalist nations, led by the United States) and believers in command economies (the communist bloc, led by the Soviet Union).

The US and USSR never went to war against each other directly, but dozens of smaller (yet still tragic and significant) wars unfolded around the world as bitter fights over economic systems turned bloody. Korea, Vietnam, Nicaragua, Afghanistan, Angola... millions of people died in the various "hot" theaters of a Cold War fought to decide whether markets or states should control economic affairs.

After reading activity

1. ***True or false.***

1) In traditional economic systems, people doing business according to the local traditional and people are not willing to accept new ideas.

2) Private property is subjected to the management of the whole community in all traditional economic systems.

3) In command economies, people cannot have any private possessions.

4) In a market economy, government doesn't exist.

5) The conflicts of social political systems are actually a disagreement of the way to allocate the natural resources between people.

2. ***Discussion.***

1) In the late nineteenth century, USA was close to a pure market economy, but it practices mixed economic system now. Why did USA abandon the laissez-faire? What are the advantages and disadvantages of a pure market economy?

2) Market economies are almost always associated with democracy and capitalism. Do you agree or disagree with this statement? Take Singapore and China as examples to illustrate your points.

Kaleidoscope

A Brief Description of the Economic Systems from Selected Countries

• Australia

Australia is a wealthy country; it generates its income from various sources including mining-related exports, telecommunications, banking and manufacturing. It has a market economy, a relatively high GDP per capita, and a relatively low rate of poverty. In terms of average wealth, Australia ranked second in the world after Switzerland in 2013, although the nation's poverty rate increased from 10.2% to 11.8%, from 2000/01 to 2013. It was identified by the Credit Suisse Research Institute as the nation with the highest median wealth in the world and the second-highest average wealth per adult in 2013.

The Australian dollar is the currency for the nation, including Christmas Island, Cocos (Keeling) Islands, and Norfolk Island, as well as the independent Pacific Island states of Kiribati, Nauru, and Tuvalu. With the 2006 merger of the Australian Stock Exchange and the Sydney Futures Exchange, the Australian Securities Exchange became the ninth largest in the world.

Ranked third in the Index of Economic Freedom (2010), Australia is the world's twelfth largest economy and has the fifth highest per capita GDP (nominal) at $66,984. The country was ranked second in the United Nations 2011 Human Development Index and first in Legatum's 2008 Prosperity Index.

• Brazil

Brazil is the largest national economy in Latin America, the world's eight largest economy at market exchange rates and the seventh largest in purchasing power parity (PPP), according to the International Monetary Fund and the World Bank. Brazil has a mixed economy with abundant natural resources. The Brazilian economy has been predicted to become one of the five largest in the world in the decades to come, the GDP per capita following and growing, provided that large investments in productivity gains are made to substitute the GDP growth of the last decade that is attributable to the increase in the number of people working. Its current GDP per capita is $15,153 in 2014, putting Brazil in the 77th position according to IMF data. Active in agricultural, mining, manufacturing and service sectors Brazil has a labor force of over a 107 million (ranking 6th worldwide) and unemployment of 6.2% (ranking 64th worldwide).

The country has been expanding its presence in international financial and commodities markets, and is one of a group of four emerging economies called the BRIC countries. Brazil has been the world's largest producer of coffee for the last 150 years. It has become the fourth largest car market in the world. Major export products include aircraft, electrical equipment, automobiles, ethanol, textiles, footwear, iron ore, steel, coffee, orange juice, soybeans and corned beef. In total, Brazil ranks 23rd worldwide in value of exports.

• France

A member of the Group of 7 (formerly G8) leading industrialised countries, as of 2014, it is ranked as the world's ninth largest and the EU's second largest economy by purchasing power parity. With 31 of the 500 biggest companies in the world in 2015, France ranks fourth in the Fortune Global 500, ahead of Germany and the UK. France joined 11 other EU members to launch the euro in 1999, with euro coins and banknotes completely replacing the French franc (₣) in 2002.

France is part of a monetary union, the Eurozone (dark blue), and of the EU single market.

France has a mixed economy that combines extensive private enterprise with substantial state enterprise and government intervention. The government retains considerable influence over key segments of infrastructure sectors, with majority ownership of railway, electricity, aircraft, nuclear power and telecommunications. It has been relaxing its control over these sectors since the early 1990s.The government is slowly corporatising the state sector and selling off holdings in France Télécom, Air France, as well as in the insurance, banking, and defence industries. France has an important aerospace industry led by the European consortium Airbus, and has its own national spaceport, the Centre Spatial Guyanais.

According to the World Trade Organization (WTO), in 2009 France was the world's sixth largest exporter and the fourth largest importer of manufactured goods. In 2008, France was the third largest recipient of foreign direct investment among OECD countries at $118 billion, ranking behind Luxembourg (where foreign direct investment was essentially monetary transfers to banks located there) and the US ($316 billion), but above the UK ($96.9 billion), Germany ($25 billion), or Japan ($24 billion).

• India

According to the International Monetary Fund (IMF), the Indian economy in 2015 was nominally worth US$2.183 trillion; it is the seventh-largest economy by market exchange rates, and is, at US$8.027 trillion, the third-largest by purchasing power parity, or PPP. With its average annual GDP growth rate of 5.8% over the past two decades, and reaching 6.1% during 2011—2012, India is one of the world's fastest-growing economies. However, the country ranks 140th in the world in nominal GDP per capita and 129th in GDP per capita at PPP. Until 1991, all Indian governments followed protectionist policies that were influenced by socialist economics. Widespread state intervention and regulation largely walled the economy off from the outside world. An acute balance of payments crisis in 1991 forced the nation to liberalise its economy; since then it has slowly moved towards a free-market system by emphasizing both foreign trade and direct investment inflows. India's recent economic model is largely capitalist. India has been a member of WTO since 1 January 1995.

The 486.6-million worker Indian labour force is the world's second-largest, as of 2011. The service sector makes up 55.6% of GDP, the industrial sector 26.3% and the agricultural sector

18.1%. India's foreign exchange remittances were US$70 billion in year 2014, the largest in the world, contributed to its economy by 25 million Indians working in foreign countries. Major agricultural products include rice, wheat, oilseed, cotton, jute, tea, sugarcane, and potatoes. Major industries include textiles, telecommunications, chemicals, pharmaceuticals, biotechnology, food processing, steel, transport equipment, cement, mining, petroleum, machinery, and software. In 2006, the share of external trade in India's GDP stood at 24%, up from 6% in 1985. In 2008, india's share of world trade was 1.68%; in 2011, India was the world's tenth-largest importer and the nineteenth-largest exporter. Major exports include petroleum products, textile goods, jewellery, software, engineering goods, chemicals, and leather manufactures. Major imports include crude oil, machinery, gems, fertiliser, and chemicals. Between 2001 and 2011, the contribution of petrochemical and engineering goods to total exports grew from 14% to 42%. India was the second largest textile exporter after China in the world in calendar year 2013.

Driven by growth, India's nominal GDP per capita has steadily increased from US$329 in 1991, when economic liberalisation began, to US$1,265 in 2010, and is estimated to increase to US$2,110 by 2016; however, it has remained lower than those of other Asian developing countries such as Indonesia, Malaysia, Philippines, Sri Lanka, and Thailand, and is expected to remain so in the near future.

- **Japan**

As of 2012, Japan is the third largest national economy in the world, after the United States and China, in terms of nominal GDP, and the fourth largest national economy in the world, after the United States, China and India, in terms of purchasing power parity. As of 2014, Japan's public debt was estimated at more than 200 percent of its annual gross domestic product, the largest of any nation in the world. In August 2011, Moody's rating has cut Japan's long-term sovereign debt rating one notch from Aa3 to Aa2 inline with the size of the country's deficit and borrowing level. The large budget deficits and government debt since the 2009 global recession and followed by earthquake and tsunami in March 2011 made the rating downgrade. The service sector accounts for three quarters of the gross domestic product.

Japan's exports amounted to US$4,210 per capita in 2005. As of 2012, Japan's main export markets were China (18.1%), the United States (17.8%), South Korea (7.7%), and Thailand (5.5%). Its main exports are transportation equipment, motor vehicles, iron and steel products, semiconductors and auto parts. Japan's main import markets as of 2012 were China (21.3%), the United States (8.8%), Australia (6.4%), Saudi Arabia (6.2%), United Arab Emirates (5.0%), South Korea (4.6%) and Qatar (4.0%).

- **The United States**

The United States has a capitalist mixed economy which is fueled by abundant natural resources and high productivity. According to the International Monetary Fund, the U.S. GDP of $16.8 trillion constitutes 24% of the gross world product at market exchange rates and over 19% of the gross world product at purchasing power parity.

The US's nominal GDP is estimated to be \$17.528 trillion as of 2014. From 1983 to 2008, U.S. real compounded annual GDP growth was 3.3%, compared to a 2.3% weighted average for the rest of the G7. The country ranks ninth in the world in nominal GDP per capita and sixth in GDP per capita at PPP. The U.S. dollar is the world's primary reserve currency.

The United States is the largest importer of goods and second largest exporter, though exports per capita are relatively low. In 2010, the total U.S. trade deficit was \$635 billion. Canada, China, Mexico, Japan, and Germany are its top trading partners. In 2010, oil was the largest import commodity, while transportation equipment was the country's largest export. Japan is the largest foreign holder of U.S. public debt. The largest holder of the U.S. debt are American entities, including federal government accounts and the Federal Reserve, who hold the majority of the debt.

In 2009, the private sector was estimated to constitute 86.4% of the economy, with federal government activity accounting for 4.3% and state and local government activity (including federal transfers) the remaining 9.3%. The number of employees at all levels of government outnumber those in manufacturing by 1.7 to 1. While its economy has reached a postindustrial level of development and its service sector constitutes 67.8% of GDP, the United States remains an industrial power.

Mini-case Study

The EU Grounds the GE-Honeywell Merger

Political and legal differences around the world can hit home and restrict strategic alliances even between two domestic companies. We have entered the era of global reach of regulatory bodies.

General Electric and Honeywell—two American corporations—had planned the \$41 billion deal and gained approval from the Department of Justice in the United States. But the European Commission, the executive arm of the EU, has jurisdiction over mergers between firms with combined revenues of \$4.2 billion, of which \$212 million must be within Europe. The GE-Honeywell deal fell within these criteria. GE, for example, employs 85,000 people in Europe and had \$25 billion in revenue in 2000.

Whereas the U.S. antitrust regulation tends to focus on the potential harm to business competition. Commissioner Mario Monti's decision to block the deal in June 2001 was based largely on a concern about potential "bundling". The concern was that GE would "use its clout to tie two core products into a single package—jet engines and Honeywell avionics—and sell it at a price lower than European competitor could match". While the European Commission admitted that customers might benefit from lower prices in the short term, they were more worried about the long-run competitiveness of GE's rivals and the future of the aerospace industry. The EC wanted to remedy this potential scenario by selling off several businesses such as GE Capital Aviation Services (Gecas), a non-aircraft and leasing business. Whereas GE had suggested various structural remedies to the concerns about Gecas, the Commission remained wary about the potential effects of vertical integrations. Noel Forgeard, CEO of Airbus Industry, the European plane-maker that would have an interest in the competitive issues, said that he did not oppose the GE-Honeywell deal after discussing with Jack Welch how the deal would be structured.

Monti indicated that he would accept fewer divestments in other areas as long as he got the structural commitments he wanted regarding Gecas. At that point, however, GE is now offering to sell businesses with $1 billion in revenues—half its original offer—and has taken off the table most of Honeywell's avionics and aerospace products.

On June 14, 2001, Jack Welch, the highly successful chairman and CEO of GE, who postponed his retirement to see the deal with Honeywell to fruition, said: "We have always said there is a point at which we wouldn't do the deal. The Commission's extraordinary demands are far beyond that point. This shows you are never too old to get surprised."

Paul O'Neill, U.S. Treasury Secretary, stated that the Commission's proposal to block the deal was "off the wall... They are the closest thing you can find to an autocratic organization that can successfully impose their will on things that one would think are outside their scope of attention". However, Monti, obviously distributed by what he called attempts to bring about political intervention in the European antitrust case, later stated that the GE-Honeywell situation was a rare case of disagreement between the transatlantic competition authorities.

(Source:窦卫霖. 跨文化商务交流案例分析[M]. 北京:对外经济贸易大学出版社,2007. p.183.)

Questions

1. ***Match the names with their titles.***

Mario Monti	CEO of GE
Noel Forgeard	Commissioner of European Commission
Jack Welch	U.S. Treasury secretary
Paul O'Neill	CEO of Airbus Industry

2. ***True or false.***

1) After the merger, GE would sell its product at a high price that its European competitors hardly match.
2) European Commission blocked the deal to protect European customers' interest.
3) GE-Honeywell Merger was incompatible with American antitrust law.
4) Airbus believed European airplane companies would get benefit from the GE-Honeywell deal.
5) Paul O'Neill criticized that European Commission had had too much political intervention in the GE-Honeywell case.

3. ***Short questions.***

1) How did the Department of Justice in the U.S. and the European Commission of the European Union view the GE-Honeywell deal respectively?

2) How could European Commission's verdict have a legal binding force on the merger between two American companies?

3) Why did not GE accept European Commission's suggestions about reconstructing the commitments in the deal?

After-class Exercises

Reading

(1)

Campus Collaboration: Foreign Universities Find Working in China Harder than They Expected

From *The Economist*, Jan. 5th 2013

Whether for the narrow purpose of generating revenue or the broader goal of engaging more deeply with a rapidly emerging and ever more important nation, foreign universities are scrambling to recruit in China as well as to establish or expand their presence there.

Britain's Lancaster University, New York's Juilliard School, which specialises in music, and Duke University in North Carolina, are just the latest foreign institutions to pile into an already crowded marketplace. Other co-operative and exchange programmes in higher education are being announced almost every month. Some recruit Chinese students to foreign universities, or foreign students to Chinese ones. Others take the form of research facilities or academic-exchange centres. Some offer dual degrees. The most ambitious involve building, staffing and operating satellite campuses in China.

None of them finds it easy to work with an academic system whose standards and values are so different from those in the West. The collapse of a Beijing-based undergraduate programme jointly run by two elite institutions—Yale University in America and Peking University—has highlighted some of the difficulties that foreigners face. Yale's administrators pulled the plug in July, citing high expenses, low enrolment and weaknesses in its Chinese-language programme.

In 2007 less than a year after the programme was launched, a visiting Yale faculty member, Stephen Stearns, wrote an open letter complaining about the rampant plagiarism he claimed was being committed by many of his Chinese students. "When a student I am teaching steals words and ideas from an author without acknowledgment, I feel cheated," said Mr Stearns. "I ask myself, why should I teach people who knowingly deceive me?"

However, Yale's experience has not deterred others from coming in, with strong encouragement from the Chinese government. Officials hope such ventures will stop academic talent moving abroad, and push Chinese universities to improve. But plagiarism, false credentials and research, and cheating on tests, remain obstacles for foreign universities in China.

In the past year the number of Chinese institutions participating in Arizona State's dual-degree programme, which allows participating students to gain an American and a Chinese degree, has risen from 3 to 33. About 95% of students achieve the grades they need to enter the fifth year of study that results in a master's degree from Arizona State.

That high success rate, Mr Simon says, requires heavy investment in sending academic staff to China to screen candidates. "We want high-quality people with good English and the ability to pay. Given the level of fraud and fake documents, it is worth the big investment it takes for us to do it this way," he says.

Foreign scholars collaborating with institutions in China sometimes fret about how to handle sensitive topics or curriculum materials. Dali Yang, who heads a research and conference centre in Beijing run by the University of Chicago, says there are few political constraints on the workshops or classes he organises. Even for public events, he says he does not try to deter academics who work on such sensitive topics as population-control policies. But he suggests a need for academics to be cautious. "They have good judgment and know to be respectful of what goes on here. That doesn't mean they have to shut up, but they know it won't go well if they go so far that Chinese counterparts won't be able to participate," he says.

In November Lee Bollinger, the president of Columbia University in New York, said his institution's academic centre in Beijing, which opened in 2009, would uphold academic "freedom and openness". He added that if anything threatened to compromise its "fundamental values", Columbia would have to leave China.

Questions

1. How many types of formats are there when a foreign educational institution enters into the Chinese market?
2. What challenges do foreign universities encounter in China?
3. What make Yale University end their education project in China?
4. What is Chinese government's attitude towards higher-education collaboration with foreign universities?
5. What remain the main obstacles for foreign institutions in China?
6. How can Arizona State University make such a big success in the Chinese academic culture?
7. Does Mr. Yang feel his teaching hardly compatible with the Chinese academic system?
8. How do you see the joint-venture educational programmes in China? Thinking back of the *Pre-class Activity*, what advices can you give to that foreign institution now?

(2)

The Confucian Renaissance

By Todd Crowell

In his 19th-century classic, *The Protestant Ethic and the Spirit of Capitalism*, German sociologist Max Weber argued that Asian values were incompatible with the development of a modern economic system. He saw in the brand of Christianity practiced in northern Europe the only ethical system with the attributes needed to make capitalism work.

At the beginning of the 20th century, many Asian intellectuals might have agreed with him. Commenting on Confucianism, the Chinese leftist thinker, Chen Duxiu, said in 1916, "If we want to build a new society on the Western model in order to survive in the world, we must courageously throw away that which is incompatible with the new belief, the new society, the new state."

History, of course, has proved Weber and Chen wrong. It is now plain that the most dynamic practitioners of capitalism at the dawn of the 21st century are to be found in Asia. More strikingly, all of them are located within what might be called a Confucian cultural zone.

It is clear the success of Japan and the "Four Tigers" (Korea, Taiwan of China, Hong Kong of China and Singapore) owe much to such essential Confucian precepts as self-discipline, social harmony, strong families and a reverence for education. That has led to unprecedented and increasingly broad-based international interest in the creed. Yet the Confucian renaissance may only be in its early phases.

For most of the last century, Confucius (or Kongfuzi; Master Kong) has been under a cloud in his homeland. But recently, Beijing's leaders have begun to characterize the sage's philosophy as a national treasure that will benefit today's Chinese.

September's official celebration of the birth of Confucius was the biggest since the People's Republic of China was established in 1949. The state-owned television broadcast festivities observing his 2,556th birthday on September 28 on a scale never before seen in China. More than 2,500, including many fairly high-ranking Communist Party cadres, made a pilgrimage to the philosopher's birthplace at Qufu in Shandong province.

The latest government line is that Confucianism can serve as a moral foundation to help build a more "harmonious society" in keeping with the efforts to address social problems such as the polarization of society and a wide spread "money first" mentality.

It is little surprise that Chinese leaders are seeking to rehabilitate their country's most famous and influential thinker. Confucianism can help provide the nation with a much-needed ethical anchor. Of all the world's great canons, Confucianism is the most practical. What concerned him most were people's relationships with one another and with the state. He also focused on social justice and good government. *Ren* or benevolence was the pillar of the master's thought.

Another was learning. Whether East Asian countries include *The Analects* (sayings of

Confucius) in their social curricula, they all understand that education is the root of national strength and prosperity. The ingrained respect for knowledge—and for the teacher who imparts it—is the key factor in the outstanding academic performance of East Asians on a global basis.

Yet the long-time preoccupation with reciting the Nine Classics (ancient musical pieces) has also produced educational systems in Asia that stress memorization at the expense of creative thinking. This is a distortion of Confucian philosophy, which emphasized both knowledge and thought. The master said: "He who does not think is lost. He who thinks but does not learn is in great danger."

To the master, the family was fundamental to the social order. "If the family is properly regulated, the state will be too," he reasoned. No amount of legislation, Confucius taught, could either take the family's place or perform its function as the linchpin of a well-ordered society. In the master's world, children defer to parents, wives to their husbands and subjects to rulers in a natural progression.

In return for the loyalty of subjects, Confucius demanded that a ruler display benevolence and unstintingly serve their interests. If he didn't, citizens had the right to remonstrate. Mencius, the second-most influential Confucian philosopher, later developed the concept of a "divine right of rebellion". If an emperor became a tyrant, he would lose the mandate of heaven and people would overthrow him. Today they might simply throw the leader out of office in an election. Confucius and democracy are not incompatible.

Throughout history, the rigid and unthinking application of Confucian principles repeatedly produced complacent closed societies that were unable to make progress. They paid a terrible price: foreign subjugation and internal upheaval. Modern Confucians must guard against repeating such mistakes. If they succeed in adapting their time-tested heritage to contemporary challenges, Master Kong's teaching may blossom beyond East Asia to enrich all mankind in the next century.

Questions

1. How do Max Web and Chen Duxiu think about the compatibility between Confucianism and modern economy?
2. What is Confucian cultural zone?
3. What is the relevance of Confucianism in modern China?
4. How does Confucianism help to establish Chinese education system?
5. According to the writer, is Confucianism compatible with democracy?
6. Once Confucian ethic system was blamed for causing the backwardness and weakness of China, but now more scholars contribute the fast economic development in the East Asia to Confucianism. Is that saying Confucianism fit the modern time better than the ancient time? If not, why? What cause the backwardness of the ancient China, and what help to boost a blooming East Asian economy?

More research projects

1. Interview a foreign student in your university to learn about the educational system in his or her country and the relationship between educational training and positions in business and society.
2. Research the marriage and family system of a country of your choice and make comparisons with the family life style in China.

UNIT 4 Cultural Patterns

Pre-class Activity

Gentlemen First

An American couple went to an upscale Western restaurant with their friends who came to China for a short visit. When they sat down, the Chinese waiter poured water for the male guest first, served the host second, and then poured for the ladies last. As he started pouring, the American guest indicated that he should serve the ladies first, but to no avail. When the appetizers arrived, the waiter again tried to serve the gentlemen before the ladies. The American guest became quite angry with the waiter. He said to him sharply, "Please serve the ladies first."

***Please work in groups and discuss following questions*:**

(1) What are the values American guests hold?

(2) What values does the Chinese waiter believe?

(3) Have you observed similar hierarchy in other social context, like workplace or school? If you have, describe the situation you witnessed or involved.

Read to Learn More

Text

Hofstede's Cultural Taxonomy

By Myron W. Lustig & Jolene Koester

Geert Hofstede's impressive studies of cultural differences in value orientations offer another approach to understanding the range of cultural differences. Hofstede's approach is based on the assertion that people carry mental programs, or "software of the mind", that are developed during childhood and are reinforced by their culture. These mental programs contain the ideas of a culture and are expressed through its dominant values. To identify the principal values of different cultures, Hofstede initially surveyed more than 100, 000 IBM employees in 71 countries, and he has subsequently broadened his analysis to include many others.

Through theoretical reasoning and statistical analyses, Hofstede's early research identified five dimensions along which dominant patterns of a culture can be ordered: power distance, uncertainty avoidance, individualism versus collectivism, masculinity versus femininity, and long-term versus short-term orientation to time. Recently two additional dimensions have been added: indulgence versus restraint and monumentalism versus self-effacement. Hofstede's work provides an excellent synthesis of the relationships between cultural values and social behaviours.

Power Distance

One of the basic concerns of all cultures is the issue of human inequality. Contrary to the claim in the U.S. *Declaration of Independence* that "all men are created equal", all people in a culture do not have equal levels of status or social power. Depending on the culture, some people might be regarded as superior to others because of their wealth, age, gender, education, physical strength, birth order, personal achievements, family background, occupation, or a wide variety of other characteristics.

Cultures also differ in the extent to which they view such status inequalities as good or bad, right or wrong, just or unjust, and fair or unfair. That is, all cultures have particular value orientations about the appropriateness or importance of status differences and social hierarchies. Thus power distance refers to the degree to which the culture believes that institutional and organizational power should be distributed unequally and the decisions of the power holders should be challenged or accepted.

Cultures that prefer small power distances—such as Austria, Denmark, Israel, and New Zealand—believe in the importance of minimizing social or class inequalities, questioning or challenging authority figures, reducing hierarchical organizational structures, and using power only for legitimate purposes. Conversely, cultures that prefer large power distances—such as those in Arab countries, Guatemala, Malaysia, and the Philippines—believe that each person has a rightful and protected place in the social order, that the actions of authorities should not be challenged or questioned, that hierarchy and inequality are appropriate and beneficial, and that those with social status have a right to use their power for whatever purposes and in whatever ways they deem desirable.

The consequences of the degree of power distance that a culture prefers are evident in family customs, the relationships between students and teachers, organizational practices, and in other areas of social life. Even the language systems in high power-distance cultures emphasize distinctions based on a social hierarchy.

Children raised in high power-distance cultures are expected to obey their parents without challenging or questioning them, while children raised in low power-distance cultures put less value on obedience and are taught to seek reasons or justifications for their parents' action. Even the language of high power-distance cultures is more sensitive to hierarchical distinctions; Chinese and Korean languages, for instance, have separate terms for older brother, younger brother, younger sister, older sister, and so on.

Students in high power-distance cultures are expected to comply with the wishes and requests of their teachers, and conformity is regarded very favorably. As a consequence, the curriculum in these cultures is likely to involve a great deal of rote learning, and students are discouraged from asking questions because questions might pose a threat to the teacher's authority. In low power-distance cultures, students regard their independence as very important, and they are less likely to conform to the expectations of teachers or other authorities. The educational system itself reinforces the low-power values by teaching students to ask questions, to solve problems creatively and uniquely, and to challenge the evidence leading to conclusion.

In the business world, managers in high power-distance cultures are likely to prefer an autocratic or centralized decision-making style, whereas subordinates in these cultures expect and want to be closely supervised. Alternatively, managers in low power-distance cultures prefer a consultative or participative decision-making style, and their subordinates expect a great deal of autonomy and independence as they do their work.

European Americans tend to have a relatively low power distance, though it is by no means exceptionally low. However, when European Americans communicate with people from cultures that value a relatively large power distance, problems related to differences in expectations are likely. For example, European American exchange students in a South American or Asian culture sometimes have difficulty adapting to a world in which people are expected to do as they are told without questioning the reasons for the requests. Conversely, exchange students visiting the United States from high power-distance cultures sometimes feel uneasy because they expect their teachers to direct and supervise their work closely, but they may also have been taught that it would be rude and impolite to ask for the kinds of information that might allow them to be more successful.

Uncertainty Avoidance

Another concern of all cultures is how they will adapt to changes and cope with uncertainties. The future will always be unknown in some respects. This unpredictability and the resultant anxiety that inevitably occurs are basic in human experience.

Cultures differ in the extent to which they prefer and can tolerate ambiguity and, therefore, in the means they select for coping with change. Thus, all cultures differ in their perceived need to be changeable and adaptable. Hofstede refers to these variations as the uncertainty avoidance dimension, the extent to which the culture feels threatened by ambiguous, uncertain situations and tries to avoid them by establishing more structure.

At one extreme on this dimension are cultures such as those of Denmark, Jamaica, Ireland, and Singapore, which are all low in uncertainty avoidance and therefore have a high tolerance for uncertainty and ambiguity. They believe in minimizing the number of rules and rituals that govern social conduct and human behavior, in accepting and encouraging dissent among cultural members, in tolerating people who behave in ways that are considered socially deviant, and in taking risks and trying new things. Conversely, the cultures of Greece, Guatemala, Portugal and Uruguay are among those that prefer to avoid uncertainty as a cultural value. They desire or even demand consensus about societal goals, and they do not like to tolerate dissent or allow deviation in the behaviors of cultural members. They try to ensure certainty and security through an extensive set of rules, regulations, and rituals.

Cultures must cope with the need to create a world that is more certain and predictable, and they do so by inventing rules and rituals to constrain human behaviors. Because members of high uncertainty-avoidance cultures tend to be worried about the future, they have high levels of anxiety and are highly resistant to change. They regard the uncertainties of life as a continuous threat that must be overcome. Consequently, these cultures develop many rules to control social behaviors, and they often adopt elaborate rituals and religious practices that have a precise form or sequence.

Members of low uncertainty-avoidance cultures tend to live day to day, and they are more willing to accept change and take risks. Conflict and competition are natural; dissent is acceptable; deviance is not threatening; and individual achievement is regarded as beneficial. Consequently, these cultures need few rules to control social behaviors, and they are unlikely to adopt religious rituals that require precise patterns of enactment.

Differences in level of uncertainty avoidance can result in unexpected problems in intercultural communication. For instance, European Americans tend to have a moderately low level of uncertainty avoidance. When these U. S. Americans communicate with someone from a high uncertainty-avoidance culture, such as those in Japan or France, they are likely to be seen as too nonconforming and unconventional, and they may view their Japanese or French counterparts as rigid and overly controlled. Conversely, when these U.S. Americans communicate with someone from an extremely low uncertainty-avoidance cultures, such as the Irish or Swedes, they are likely to be viewed as too structured and uncompromising, whereas they may perceive their Irish or Swedish counterparts as too willing to accept dissent.

Individualism versus Collectivism

Another concern of all cultures, and a problem for which they must all find a solution, involves people's relationships to the larger social groups of which they are a part. People must live and interact together for the culture to survive. In doing so, they must develop way of relating that strikes a balance between showing concern for themselves and concern for others.

Cultures differ in the extent to which individual autonomy is regarded favorably or unfavorably. Thus, cultures vary in their tendency to encourage people to be unique and independent or conforming and interdependent. Hofstede refers to these variations as the individualism-collectivism dimension, the degree to which a culture relies on and has allegiance to the self or the group.

Highly individualistic cultures, such as the dominant cultures in Austria, Belgium, the Netherlands, and the United States, believe that people are only supposed to take care of themselves and perhaps their immediate families. In individualist cultures, the autonomy of the individual is paramount. Key words used to invoke this cultural pattern include *independence*, *privacy*, *self*, and the all-important *I*. Decisions are based on what is good for the individual, not for the group, because the person is the primary source of motivation. Similarly, a judgment about what is right or wrong can be made only from the point of view of each individual.

Cultures such as those in Guatemala, Indonesia, Pakistan, and West Africa value a collectivist orientation. They require an absolute loyalty to the group, though the relevant group might be as varied as the nuclear family, the extended family, a caste, or a jati (a subgrouping of a caste). In collectivist cultures, decisions that juxtapose the benefits to the individual and the benefits to the group are always based on what is best for the group, and the groups to which a person belongs are the most important social units. In turn, the group is expected to look out for and take care of its individual members. Consequently, collectivist cultures believe in obligations to the group, dependence of the individual on organizations and institutions, a "we" consciousness, and an emphasis on belonging.

Huge cultural differences can be explained by differences on the individualism-collectivism dimension. We have already noted that collectivistic cultures tend to be group-oriented. A related characteristic is that they typically impose a very large psychological distance between those who are members of their group (the ingroup) and those who are not (the outgroup). Ingroup members are required to have unquestioning loyalty, whereas outgroup members are regarded as almost inconsequential. Conversely, members of individualistic cultures do not perceive a large chasm between ingroup and outgroup members; ingroup members are not as close, but outgroup members are not as distant. Scholars such as Harry Triandis believe that individualism-collectivism dimension is by far the most important attribute that distinguishes one culture from another; thus, it has been extensively researched.

Individualist cultures train their members to speak out as a means of resolving difficulties. In classroom, students from individualistic cultures are likely to ask questions of the teacher; students from collectivistic cultures are not. Similarly, people from individualistic cultures are more likely than those from collectivistic cultures to use confrontational strategies when dealing with interpersonal problems; those with a collectivistic orientation are likely to use avoidance, third-party intermediaries, or other face-saving techniques. Indeed, a common maxim among European Americans, who are highly individualistic, is that "the squeaky wheel gets the grease" (suggesting that one should make noise in order to be rewarded); the corresponding maxim among the Japanese, who are somewhat collectivistic, is "the nail that sticks up gets pounded" (so one should always try to blend in).

Masculinity versus Femininity

A fourth concern of all cultures, and for which they must all find solutions, pertains to gender expectations and the extent to which people prefer achievement and assertiveness or nurturance and social support. Hofstede refers to these variations as the masculinity-femininity dimension. This dimension indicates the degree to which a culture values "masculine" behaviors, such as assertiveness and the acquisition of wealth, or "feminine" behaviors, such as caring for others and the quality of life.

At one extreme are masculine cultures such as those in Austria, Italy, Japan, and Mexico, which believe in achievement and ambition. In this view, people should be judged on their performance, and those who achieve have the right to display the material goods they acquired. The people in masculine cultures also believe in ostentatious manliness, and very specific behaviors and products are associated with appropriate male behavior.

At the other extreme are feminine cultures such as those of Chile, Portugal, Sweden, and Thailand, which believe less in external achievements and shows of manliness and more in the importance of life choices that improve intrinsic aspects of the quality of life, such as service to others and sympathy for the unfortunate. People in these feminine cultures are also likely to prefer equality between the sexes, less prescriptive role behaviors associated with each gender, an acceptance of nurturing roles for both women and men.

Members of highly masculine cultures believe that men should be assertive and women should be nurturing. Sex roles are clearly differentiated, and sexual inequality is regarded as beneficial. The reverse is true for members of highly feminine cultures: men are far less interested in achievement, sex roles are far more fluid, and equality between the sexes is the norm.

Teachers in masculine cultures praise their best students because academic performance is rewarded highly. Similarly, male students in these masculine cultures strive to be competitive, visible, successful, and vocationally oriented. In feminine cultures, teachers rarely praise individual achievements and academic performance because social accommodation is more highly regarded. Male students try to cooperate with one another and develop a sense of solidarity; they try to behave modestly and properly; they select subjects because they are intrinsically interesting rather than vocationally rewarding, and friendliness is much more important than brilliance.

Long-Term versus Short-Term Time Orientation

A fifth concern of all cultures is its orientation to time. Hofstede has acknowledged that the four previously described dimensions have a Western bias, as they were developed by scholars from Europe or the United States who necessarily brought to their work an implicit set of assumptions and categories about the types of cultural values they would likely find. His time-orientation dimension is based on the work of Michael H. Bond, a Canadian who has lived in Asia for the past thirty years and who assembled a large team of researchers from Hong Kong and Taiwan to develop and administer a Chinese Value Survey to university students around the world.

The time-orientation dimension refers to a person's point of reference about life and work. Cultures that promote a long-term orientation toward life admire persistence, thriftiness, and humility. Linguistic and social distinctions between elder and younger siblings are common, and deferred gratification of needs is widely accepted. Conversely, cultures with a short-term orientation toward changing events have an expectation of quick results following one's actions. The Chinese, for example, typically have a long-term time orientation—note the tendency to mark time in year-long increments, as in the Year of the Dragon or the Year of the Dog—whereas Europeans typically have a short-term time orientation and aggregate time in month-long intervals (such as Aries, Gemini,

Pisces, or Aquarius).

Indulgence versus Restraint

Recently Hofstede has included two additional dimensions to those previously described. Based on recent research, including ideas from Middle Eastern, Nordic, and Eastern European perspectives, Hofstede has added the dimensions of indulgence versus restraint and monumentalism versus self-effacement.

The indulgence versus restraint dimension juxtaposes hedonism with self-discipline. Cultures high on indulgence encourage pleasure, enjoyment, spending, consumption, sexual, gratification, and general merriment. Alternatively, cultures high on restraint encourage the control of such hedonistic gratifications, and the pleasures and enjoyment associated with leisure activities are discouraged.

Monumentalism versus Self-effacement

The monumentalism versus self-effacement dimension juxtaposes stability with change. Cultures high on monumentalism encourage people to be like the monuments or statues that one commonly finds in parks or near government buildings: proud, unchangeable, upstanding, stable, and resolute. Alternatively, cultures high on self-effacement encourage humility, flexibility, adaptation to the situation, and feeling comfortable about life's paradoxes and inconsistencies.

(Source: Adapted from Lustig, M. W. & J. Koester, 2010. *Intercultural Competence: Interpersonal Communication Across Cultures*. 6th Edition. Boston: Pearson, pp. 113-121)

The following five tables show some countries or regions' ranking in Hofstede's culture scales:

Table 1

Individualism/Collectivism Values for Some Countries or Regions			
RANK	COUNTRY OR REGION	RANK	COUNTRY OR REGION
1	United States	10/11	Sweden
2	Australia	10/11	France
3	Great Britain	12	Ireland
4/5	Canada	13	Norway
4/5	Netherlands	14	Switzerland
6	New Zealand	15	Germany
7	Italy	16	South Africa
8	Belgium	17	Finland
9	Denmark	18	Austria

Continued

Individualism/Collectivism Values for Some Countries or Regions			
RANK	COUNTRY OR REGION	RANK	COUNTRY OR REGION
19	Israel	37	Hong Kong of China
20	Spain	38	Chile
21	India	39/41	Singapore
22/23	Japan	39/41	Thailand
22/23	Argentina	39/41	West Africa
24	Iran	42	Salvador
25	Jamaica	43	South Korea
26/27	Brazil	44	Taiwan of China
26/27	Arab countries	45	Peru
28	Turkey	46	Costa Rica
29	Uruguay	47/48	Pakistan
30	Greece	47/48	Indonesia
31	Philippines	49	Colombia
32	Mexico	50	Venezuela
33/35	Yugoslavia	51	Panama
33/35	Portugal	52	Ecuador
33/35	East Africa	53	Guatemala
36	Malaysia		

The lower the number the more the country or region promotes individualism. A higher number means the country or region can be classified as collective.

Table 2

Uncertainty Avoidance Values for Some Countries and Regions			
RANK	COUNTRY OR REGION	RANK	COUNTRY OR REGION
1	Greece	28	Ecuador
2	Portugal	29	Germany
3	Guatemala	30	Thailand
4	Uruguay	31/32	Iran
5/6	Belgium	31/32	Finland
5/6	Salvador	33	Switzerland
7	Japan	34	West Africa
8	Yugoslavia	35	Netherlands
9	Peru	36	East Africa
10/15	Spain	37	Australia
10/15	Argentina	38	Norway
10/15	Panama	39/40	South Africa
10/15	France	39/40	New Zealand
10/15	Chile	41/42	Indonesia
10/15	Costa Rica	41/42	Canada
16/17	Turkey	43	United States
16/17	South Korea	44	Philippines
18	Mexico	45	India
19	Israel	46	Malaysia
20	Colombia	47/48	Great Britain
21/22	Venezuela	47/48	Ireland
21/22	Brazil	49/50	Hong Kong of China
23	Italy	49/50	Sweden
24/25	Pakistan	51	Denmark
24/25	Austria	52	Jamaica
26	Taiwan of China	53	Singapore
27	Arab Countries		

The lower the number the more the country or region can be classified as one that does not like uncertainty. A higher number is associated with a country or region that does not feel uncomfortable with uncertainty.

Table 3

Power Distance Values for Some Countries and Regions

RANK	COUNTRY OR REGION	RANK	COUNTRY OR REGION
1	Malaysia	27/28	South Korea
2/3	Guatemala	29/30	Iran
2/3	Panama	29/30	Taiwan of China
4	Philippines	31	Spain
5/6	Mexico	32	Pakistan
5/6	Venezuela	33	Japan
7	Arab countries	34	Italy
8/9	Ecuador	35/36	Argentina
8/9	Indonesia	35/36	South Africa
10/11	India	37	Jamaica
10/11	West Africa	38	United States
12	Yugoslavia	39	Canada
13	Singapore	40	Netherlands
14	Brazil	41	Australia
15/16	France	42/44	Costa Rica
15/16	Hong Kong of China	42/44	Germany
17	Colombia	42/44	Great Britain
18/19	Salvador	45	Switzerland
18/19	Turkey	46	Finland
20	Belgium	47/48	Norway
21/23	East Africa	47/48	Sweden
21/23	Peru	49	Ireland
21/23	Thailand	50	New Zealand
24/25	Chile	51	Denmark
24/25	Portugal	52	Israel
26	Uruguay	53	Austria
27/28	Greece		

The lower the number the more the country or region can be classified as one that has a large power distance. A higher number is associated with a country or region that demonstrates small power distance.

Table 4

Masculinity Values for Some Countries and Regions			
RANK	COUNTRY OR REGION	RANK	COUNTRY OR REGION
1	Japan	28	Singapore
2/3	Austria	29	Israel
2/3	Venezuela	30/31	Indonesia
4/5	Italy	30/31	West Africa
4/5	Switzerland	32/33	Turkey
6	Mexico	32/33	Taiwan of China
7/8	Ireland	34	Panama
7/8	Jamaica	35/36	Iran
9/10	Great Britain	35/36	France
9/10	Germany	37/38	Spain
11/12	Philippines	37/38	Peru
11/12	Colombia	39	East Africa
13/14	South Africa	40	Salvador
13/14	Ecuador	41	South Korea
15	United States	42	Uruguay
16	Australia	43	Guatemala
17	New Zealand	44	Thailand
18/19	Greece	45	Portugal
18/19	Hong Kong of China	46	Chile
20/21	Argentina	47	Finland
20/21	India	48/49	Yugoslavia
22	Belgium	48/49	Costa Rica
23	Arab countries	50	Denmark
24	Canada	51	Netherlands
25/26	Malaysia	52	Norway
25/26	Pakistan	53	Sweden
27	Brazil		

The lower the number the more the country or region can be classified as one that favors masculine traits; a higher score indicates a country or region that prefers feminine traits.

(Source: Adapted from Geert Hofstede. 2001. *Cultures Consequences: Comparing Values, Behavior, Institutions and Organizations Across Nations*. 2nd ed. CA: Sage Publications.)

After reading activity

1. ***Fill in the table with information from the text. The first one has been completed as an example.***

Hofstede's Cultural Patterns	Value Description	High Score	Low Score	Countries
Power Distance	The degree to which the culture believes that institutional and organizational power should be distributed unequally and the decisions of the power holders should be challenged or accepted	Believing that each person has a rightful and protected place in the social order, that the actions of authorities should not be challenged or questioned, that hierarchy and inequality are appropriate and beneficial, and that those with social status have a right to use their power for whatever purposes and in whatever ways they deem desirable	Believing in the importance of minimizing social or class inequalities, questioning or challenging authority figures, reducing hierarchical organizational structures, and using power only for legitimate purposes	H: Arab countries, Guatemala, Malaysia, and the Philippines L: Austria, Denmark, Israel, and New Zealand
Uncertainty Avoidance				
Individualism VS Collectivism				
Masculinity VS Femininity				
Long-term VS Short-term Orientation				
Indulgence VS Restraint				
Monumentalism VS Self-Effacement				

2. ***Use Hofstede's cultural dimensions to analyze the story in the Pre-Class activity.***

3. ***Essay-writing.***

The Hofstede Centre offers a range of cultural tools based on Hofstede's research. The bar chart below is the result of the Chinese culture through the lens of the 6-D Model by using Country Comparison Tool. Write a short essay to illustrate the chart, supporting your claim with specific examples.

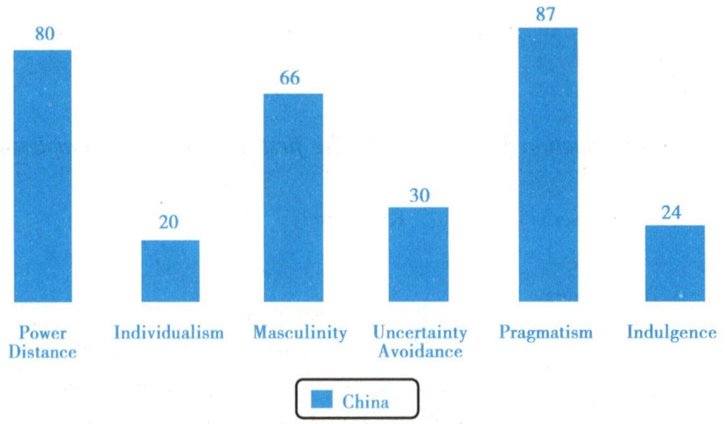

Kaleidoscope

Cultural patterns are systems of beliefs and values that work in combination to provide a coherent, if not always consistent, model for perceiving the world. Many cultures might share a similar perception of world or conduct their life in a close manner, so they could be grouped into the same cultural pattern. But one should always bear in mind that the dominant values of a culture may not be the values of all individuals within that culture.

More cultural patterns are available here for your reference.

The Kluckhohns and Strodtbeck's Value Orientations

Orientation	Values and Behavior		
Human nature: What is the basic nature of people?	Basically evil: Most people can't be trusted. People are basically bad and need to be controlled.	Mixture of good and evil: There are both evil people and good people in the world, and you have to check people out to find out which they are. People can be changed with the right guidance.	Basically good: Most people are basically pretty good at heart; they are born good.
Humankind and nature: What is the appropriate relationship between human and nature?	People subjugated to nature: People really can't change nature. Life is largely determined by external forces, such as fate and genetics. What happens was meant to happen.	People in harmony with nature: Man should, in every way, live in harmony with nature.	People being the master of nature: Human challenge to conquer and control nature. Everything from air conditioning to the "green revolution" has resulted from having met this challenge.

Continued

Orientation	Values and Behavior		
Sense of time: How should we best think about time?	Past oriented: People should learn from history, draw the values they live by from history, and strive to continue past traditions into the future.	Present oriented: The present moment is everything. Let's make the most of it. Don't worry about tomorrow: enjoy today.	Future oriented: Planning and goal setting make it possible for people to accomplish miracles, to change and grow. A little sacrifice today will bring a better tomorrow.
Activity: What is the best mode of activity?	Being: It's enough to just "be". It's not necessary to accomplish great things in life to feel your life worthwhile.	Being in becoming: The main purpose for being placed on this earth is for one's own inner development.	Doing: If people work hard and apply themselves fully, their efforts will be rewarded. What a person accomplishes is a measure of his or her worth.
Social relationships: What is the best form of social organization?	Authoritarian: There is a natural order to relations, some people are born to lead; others are followers. Decisions should be made by those in charge.	Group oriented: The best way to be organized is as a group, where everyone shares in the decision process. It is important not to make important decisions alone.	Individualism: All people should have equal rights, and each should have complete control over one's own destiny. When we have to make a decision as a group it should be "one person one vote".
Source: Kluckhohn F.R. and F. L. Strodtbeck. 1960. *Variations in Value Orientations*. New York: Row and Peterson.			

The Hall's Low- and High-Context Cultures

High-Context Cultures	Low-Context Cultures
Covert and implicit	Overt and explicit
Messages internalized	Messages plainly coded
Much nonverbal coding	Details verbalized
Reactions reserved	Reactions on the surface
Distinct ingroups and outgroups	Flexible ingroups and outgroups
Strong interpersonal bonds	Fragile interpersonal bonds
Commitment high	Commitment low
Time open and flexible	Time highly organized

(Source: Lustig, M.W. & J. Koester. 2010. *Intercultural Competence: Interpersonal Communication Across Cultures*. 6th Edition. Boston: Pearson.)

Mini-case Study

Being a Boss

Most people would agree that it is good to be the boss. However, being the boss in China has some unique characteristics to it. For example, while many Western cultures allow employees to question their bosses, or even challenge them during public meeting, Chinese employees are usually very deferential and do not voice contrary opinions. And Chinese bosses are typically expected to manage top-down and to know the right strategies and all the answers. So being the boss in China has a lot of pressure attached to it!

Bryan was aware of these differences when he started working in China. During budget season, Bryan's finance team was preparing some detailed multi-year forecasts for various parts of the business. When Bryan asked one of his staff members to make a very complicated forecast, the staff agreed to do it, and then sat patiently in front of him. Bryan thought she didn't understand, so he repeated the request, but she said, "No, I understand what you want. But I need you to tell me what the right answer is, so that I can make the forecast correctly." When Bryan told her that he didn't know the answer, she laughed and continued to sit there waiting. So, finally, Bryan said, "Of course I know the answer, but I want to see how close your calculations are, and I'll tell you afterwards how well you did." With that, she returned to her desk and got to work.

Two days later, she returned with a very well-done projection, and Bryan complimented her on the analysis. She then asked: "So, was I right?" Bryan had already forgotten their earlier conversation, but quickly remembered and told her: "Yes, you were very close."

(Adapted from Ellis.Y. S. & Bryan D. Ellis. 2012. *101 Stories for Foreigners to Understand Chinese People*. Beijing: China Intercontinental Press.)

Questions

1. How do Americans and Chinese employees act differently in a meeting?
2. Why didn't the Chinese employee leave even when she fully understood her boss's request?
3. What did Bryan learn from this experience?
4. What kinds of cultural values conduct American boss and Chinese employee here in this case? Can you fit these values and behavior with one or more cultural patterns you have just learned?

After-class Exercises

1. ***Writing.***

The graph below shows a comparison between China and the United States in 6 dimensions of culture values. Write a short composition to describe the information given below.

China in comparison with the United states

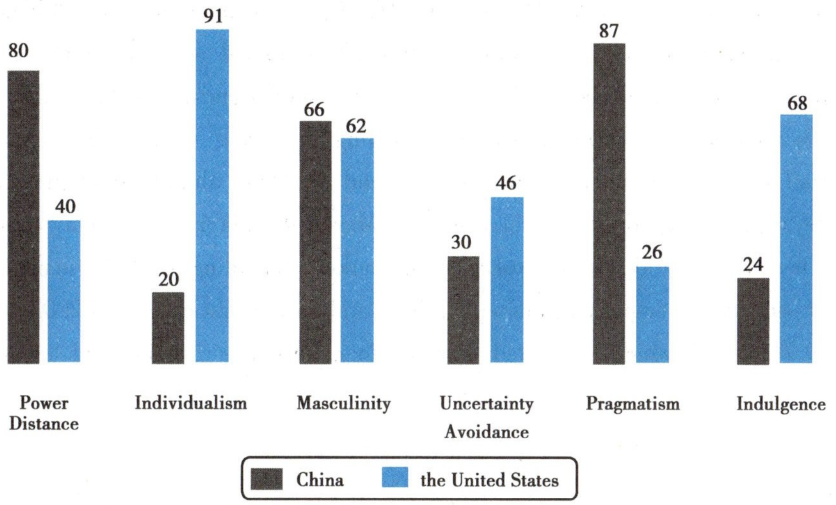

2. ***Case research project.***

There are three cases of unsuccessful business operation as listed below. Search more of its background information and work out an investigation report on the cultural reasons behind the failure of cooperation. You should apply the culture dimension theories into your analysis.

(1) Disneyland Paris

Disneyland Paris, originally Euro Disney Resort, is an entertainment resort in Marne-la-Vallée, a new town located 32 km east of the center of Paris. It opened in 1992. A second theme park, Walt Disney Studios Park opened in 2002. Mickey Mouse is a popular American cartoon figure welcomed worldwide, however, from the very beginning of the building of Disneyland Paris, the theme park has faced endless critics. A journalist in the center right French newspaper Le Figaro wrote, "I wish with all my heart that the rebels would set fire to [Euro] Disneyland." Ariane Mnouchkine, a Parisian stage director, named the concept a "cultural Chernobyl". In 2002, both parks suffered a decline of the number of tourists by 5.3%. To September, 2002, the loss was as high as 6.6 billion US dollars.

(2) Wal-Mart in Germany

Wal-Mart entered the German market when it bought 21 Wertauf hypermarkets at the end of 1997 and 74 Interspar hypermarkets a year later. However, over years, its German operations were not profitable. "They've been losing money there for years," said Robert Buchanan, head of retail analysis at A.G. Edwards & Sons. Since the late 1990s, the company had faced a great challenge of annual losses ranged between 100 million euros and 200 million euros. In 2006, it planned to sell its 85 stores in Germany to rival Metro AG, ending a nearly decade-long effort by the world's largest retailer to crack the market in Europe's biggest economy.

(3) The T&A Joint-venture merger

TCL & Alcatel Mobile Phones Limited (TAMP) was jointly set by TCL Communication

Technology Holdings Limited (TCL Communication) and Alcated, a Paris-based French telecommunication company, in August 31st, 2004. It was the first time that Chinese company expanded its mobile phone business worldwide. At that time, TCL Communication and Alcatel believed that the merger could win more competitive advantages through combined strength in the global market. Unfortunately, this cooperation ended with a huge loss of profits and brain drain. Almost all of the marketing personnel in the three main locations—Beijing, Shanghai, and Zhejiang—and more than half of the staff in sales left the company. By the end of 2004, almost all of the former Alcatel employees, at senior managerial level, had left. On May 17th, 2005, TCL finally closed down the joint venture because it could not stop losses in the market. According to TCL's financial report, the losses of T&A subsidiary company in France for 2004 and for the first quarter of 2005 was HK $309 million ($39.7 million) which accounted for more than 90 percent of the total losses of the joint venture.

UNIT 5 Conflicts and Adjustment of Cultural Values

Pre-class Activity

Exchange Journals: UK Culture Shock and Life-changing by Vienna

The following diary is written by Vienna, an Australian exchange student living in UK. Read it and answer the questions:

My experience of studying abroad, so far, has been a great one. It's like the United Nations just in my building—I've never been friends with so many people from other countries! The weather here leaves a lot to be desired but it makes me appreciate the sunny days, more so than when I was in Sydney. Despite coming to a fellow English-speaking country, I was not expecting to receive as much of a culture shock as I did. In one example, the locals have a tendency to go out in mini-skirts and singlet tops despite the temperature outside being −2 ℃. It seems "the coat" is what defines the visitors from the locals. The "native" people are politely reserved... until you get to a premier league match, where it all goes crazy! I am looking forward to experiencing more on campus life as the semester goes on.

Questions

1. What did Vienna think of the weather in UK? Did she like it?
2. How did local people dress up? What kind of clothes would make you easily identified as a foreigner?
3. Look for words used to describe the British in a normal way and in a rugby game. Does that image match what you know about the British?
4. How did she feel about these differences she encountered in UK?

Read to Learn More

Text

Cultural Shock

Cultural shock (commonly called culture shock) is the trauma you experience when you move into a culture different from your home culture. Cultural shock is a communication problem that involves the frustrations of not understanding the verbal and nonverbal communication of the host culture, its customs, and its value systems. Frustrations may include lack of food, unacceptable standards of cleanliness, different bathroom facilities, and fear for personal safety. Black, Gregersen, Mendenhall, and Stroh add another dimension to cultural shock. They suggest that the disruption of people's routines, which may range from getting up, eating breakfast, and going to work, creates a high degree of uncertainty that is very stressful. The more our routines are disrupted, the greater the level of anxiety and frustration. In addition, most people like predictability; for instance, they want the security of knowing how a hamburger at their favorite fast-food restaurant is going to taste. The English saying, "that song is best esteemed with which our ears are most acquainted", states the facts simply; We like to feel comfortable and be familiar with our surroundings. It is no surprise that cultural shock can cause so many problems with a person's comfort level. Losing our familiar signs, customs, norms, and behaviors can be very disturbing.

In a survey of 188 students from two Mid-South universities who had traveled or lived abroad, the greatest degree of cultural shock was reported in the lack of modern conveniences and standards of cleanliness. Other types of cultural shock showing statistical significance included attitudes toward women, nonverbal communication, clothing/business dress, family and marriage practices, housing, climate, educational system, financial problems, and values and ethical standards. The absence of conveniences (such as telephones that work, running water available 24 hours a day, or buses that run on time), which are taken for granted in the United States, is an additional source of frustration. People with strong religious ties may feel spiritually adrift without a church of their faith.

In the absence of bounty of U. S. shopping malls, supermarkets, and multiple television sets, depression may result. In addition to depression, people who experience cultural shock can become homesick, eat or drink compulsively, and even develop physical ailments. Unexplained anger and aggression toward people in the host culture are also reactions associated with cultural shock.

Cultural shock can be costly to a firm because it often results in the premature return of U.S. businesspeople working overseas. Some research shows that employees sent to work in foreign countries do not fail because they lack technical or professional competence but because they lack the ability to understand and adapt to another culture's way of life. Estimates on early return of U.S. expatriate managers reported by Ferraro ranged from 45% to 85%. More recent surveys report lower early return rates that range from 4% to 8%. When companies implement measures to combat cultural shock, such as conducting training programs for sojourners, the early return rate drops to less than 2%.

Some companies have used short-term stays of two to three months to determine an employee's potential for tolerating the culture. Sometimes these short-term projects are designed to prepare the person for a longer stay later. On other occasions, these brief trips are simply ways to use the talents of technical professionals who would be unwilling to go in the first place if it meant disrupting the professional advancement of a career-oriented spouse. Short trips are also cost-effective as the need to move the family is reduced or eliminated. Although the degree and type of cultural shock experienced by people who travel to another country for a short stay may be similar to the shock experienced by those who plan an extended visit, the strategies for coping during the short-term visit may differ.

Brislin identifies these five strategies used for coping with the new culture during short visit:

- **Unacceptance of the host culture**—The traveler simply behaves as he or she would in the home culture. No effort is made to learn the language or the customs of the host culture.
- **Substitution**—The traveler learns the appropriate responses or behaviors in the host culture and substitutes these responses or behaviors for the ones he or she would ordinarily use in the home culture.
- **Addition**—the person adds the behavior of the host culture when in the presence of the nationals but maintains the home culture behavior when with others of the same culture.
- **Synthesis**—this strategy integrates or combines elements of the two cultures, such as combining the dress of the United States and the Philippines.
- **Resynthesis**—The integration of ideas not found in either culture. An example of this strategy would be a U.S. traveler in China who chooses to eat neither American nor Chinese food but prefers Italian food.

Cultural shock generally goes through five stages: excitement or initial euphoria, crisis or disenchantment, adjustment, acceptance and reentry. Cultural shock has been visualized as being represented by a **U-curve**, with the top of the left side of the curve representing the positive beginning the crisis stage starts down the left side to the base of the U; the adjustment phase starts at the base of the curve; then acceptance moves up the right side of the curve; and reentry into the original culture is at the top of the right side of the curve. The **W-curve** theory, a theory that explains the adaptation of the reentry phase, explains that reentry actually takes the form of a second U-curve, with a repetition of the stages experienced during initial adjustment to the foreign culture.

The first stage is excitement and fascination with the new culture, which can last only a few days or several months. During this time, everything is new and different; you are fascinated with the food and the people. Sometimes this stage is referred to as the "honeymoon" stage, during which your enthusiasm for the new culture causes you to overlook minor problems, such as having to drink bottled water and the absence of central heating or air conditioning.

During the second stage, the crisis or disenchantment period, the "honeymoon" is over, and your excitement has turned to disappointment as you encounter more and more differences between your own culture and the new culture. Problems with transportation, unfamiliar foods and people who do not speak your native tongue now seem overwhelming. The practice of bargaining over the purchase price of everything, an exercise that was originally amusing, is now a constant source of irritation. Emotions of homesickness, anger, confusion, resentment, helplessness, and depression occur during the second stage. People at this stage often cope with such situation by making disparaging remarks about the culture; it is sometimes referred to as the "fight-back" technique. Others deal with this stage by leaving, either physically, emotionally, or psychologically. Those who remain may withdraw from people in the culture, refuse to learn the language, and develop coping behaviors of excessive drinking or drug use. Some individuals actually deny differences and will speak in glowing terms of the new culture. This second stage can last from a few weeks to several months.

In the third stage, the adjustment phase, you begin to accept the new culture or you return home. Those who stay will try new foods and make adjustments in behavior to accommodate the shopping lines and the long waits for public transportation. You begin to see the humor in situations and realize that a change in attitude toward the host culture will make the stay abroad more rewarding.

In the fourth phase, the acceptance or adaptation phase, you feel at home in the new culture, become involved in activities of the culture, cultivate friendships among the nationals, and feel comfortable in social situations with people from the host culture. You learn the language and may adopt the new culture's style of doing things. You even learn to enjoy some customs such as afternoon tea and the midday siesta that you will miss when you return to the home country.

The final phase is reentry shock, which can be almost as traumatic as the initial adjustment to a new culture, particularly after an extended stay abroad. Many individuals are shocked at the fact that they feel the same emotional, psychological and physical reactions they did when they entered the new culture. Reentry shock is experienced on returning to the home country and may follow the stages identified earlier: initial euphoria, crisis or disenchantment, adjustment, and acceptance or adaptation. You would at first be happy to be back in your own country but then become disenchanted as you realize that your friends are not really interested in hearing about your experiences abroad, your standard of living goes down, and you are unable to use such new skills as a foreign language or bargaining in the market. You then move into the adjustment stage as you become familiar with new technology and appreciate the abundance and variety of foods and clothing and the improved standards of cleanliness. You finally move into the acceptance stage when you feel comfortable with the mores of the home culture and find yourself returning to many of your earlier views and behaviors.

(Source: Adapted from 钱尼,马丁. 跨文化商务沟通. 英文版[M].6 版. 北京:中国人民大学出版社, 2013:pp. 73-77.)

After reading activity

1. ***There are 12 statements of psychological and physical conditions belonging to different stage of cultural shock. Discuss with your group members and allocate them along the U-curve.***

Learning new social and cultural norms
Confusion and anxiety
Curiosity for differences
Rejection of the new culture
Emphasis on cultural similarities
Autonomy and satisfaction
Confrontation with different behaviours and values
Effectiveness and comfort
Awareness and understanding of cultural differences
Respect for the new culture
Dual cultural identity
Fascination and excitement about the new culture

2. ***Discussion and presentation.***

You are the director of the Human Resource Department of an international company. A group of workers will be sent to work in U.S.A. You are told to give a one-week pre-departure orientation in order to train the workers so they can adapt to the new social life and work in a short time. Discuss with your group members and design a class schedule for the orientation. Then, share your work with other groups.

Kaleidoscope

Challenges of Adaptation

The problems facing anyone trying to adapt to a new and often quite different culture are numerous. During the adjustment period the new arrival might experience fear, feelings of being isolated, disliked, and even distrusted. A review of some of the reasons behind these feelings is an excellent first step in developing the skills needed to adapt to a new culture.

Language. It is obvious that someone living in a new culture will usually face problems associated with having to learn and use a second language. Long-term sojourners and immigrants to the United States who have not mastered English experience social isolation and are, as Leong and Chou note, forced "into fields that require less mastery of English language and less interpersonal interaction."

When we talk of problems associated with being exposed to new language, we are talking about two ideas—language acquisition and the ways of speaking unique to the new culture. Both of these can delay the adaptation process. Harper summarizes this view when she notes, "lack of language skills is a strong barrier to effective cultural adjustment and communication whereas lack of knowledge concerning the ways of speaking of a particular group will reduce the level of understanding that we can achieve with our counterparts." The person trying to adapt to and interact with a new culture must face challenges associated not only with learning a second language but also the special and unique patterns found within every language.

Disequilibrium. Successful adaptation demands a certain level of knowledge about the host country and making correct choices regarding that knowledge. Those choices can include everything from learning proper greeting behaviors (bowing, shaking hands, hugging, etc.) to deciding about eating utensils (chopsticks, knives and forks, fingers, etc.). As you would suspect, indecision creates problems. According to Kim, sojourners are "at least temporarily, in a state of disequilibrium, which is manifested in many emotional 'lows' of uncertainty, confusion, and anxiety." The condition of disequilibrium complicates the adaptation process as the sojourner experiences a high level of apprehension as he or she attempts to decide what constitutes appropriate behavior.

Ethnocentrism. What is interesting about the role of ethnocentrism in adapting to a new culture is that it moves in both directions. As we pointed out earlier in this chapter, ethnocentrism is that cultural bias that leads people to judge another culture by the standards and practices that they are most familiar with and the one where their loyalty resides—their own. This means that members of the host culture pass judgment on outsiders while the person trying to adapt cannot, or will not, expunge their home culture. Hence, they bring some ethnocentrism to the host culture. Anderson makes this process is that elements of the original culture can never be completely erased." The key to effective adaptation is for both parties to recognize the strong pull of ethnocentrism and attempt to keep it in check.

(Source: Samovar, L. A., R. E. Porter, & E.R. McDaniel. 2009. *Communication Between Cultures*. 6th ed. Beijing: Peking University Press, 352.)

Mini-case Study

Dr. Dong at International Medical Conference

My friend Dr. Dong had a wonderful chance to go to Seattle to present a paper at a professional meeting. He arrived expectant and happy and enjoyed his first days very much. At the medical conference, he felt quite confident in his area of research and was able to perform well in his presentation. But after a few days, he began to feel uncomfortable. His medical English was fine, but the social interaction skills were different, and he was unsure of the cues and the communication style.

He worried more and more that he was misunderstanding simple English greetings and table talk conventions. When someone greeted him with, "Hi, how's it going?" he thought they had asked him "where are you going?" and answered with the name of the conference hall, only to get a quizzical stare from them. At a Western style dinner, a colleague asked, "So how're you enjoying, the States?" he thought he heard, "how are you enjoying your steak?" and answered that he was eating chicken, not beef. That time, they smiled, and patiently repeated the question, then both laughed at the error. By the end of the meetings, he felt a deep sense of "cultural stress" and was worn out from having to pay attention to so many new expressions and ways of dealing with things. He felt his handshake was not as firm as 'Americans', found that people reacted unusually when he modestly insisted his English was not good after they complimented him, didn't know how to accept dinner invitations properly and therefore missed out on going to several lunches.

Dr. Dong's visit to the US was only three weeks long, but by the end of the 5-day medical conference, he was already starting to feel more confident. Sure he felt a little foolish about some of the mistakes he had made, but he quickly learned to laugh at his errors and found his colleagues smiled with him. This broke down the barriers to communication and helped him build some good professional relationships. And after the conference, he contacted the family I had referred him to and had a very nice time visiting them. By the time he returned to China, he was feeling quite positive about his American trip, and was glad for the new experiences and new skills it had given him.

Questions

1. What cultural shock did Dr. Dong experience? How many stages of cultural shock did he go through?
2. How did Dr. Dong adjust to cultural differences?
3. What do you learn from this story?

After-class Exercises

Reading

A Ride on a Roller Coaster

What happens to someone living in a different culture? The experience can be like riding a roller coaster. People can experience both elation and depression in a very short period. They can vacillate between loving and hating the new country. Often, but not always, there is an initial period when newcomers feel enthusiasm and excitement. The cultural differences they experience at first can be fascinating rather than troubling. At first, there is often a high level of interest and motivation because the newcomers are eager to become familiar with the new culture. Life seems exciting, novel, exotic, and stimulating. However, after a while, the newness and strangeness of being in another country can influence emotions in a negative way. Many people in a new culture do not realize that their problems, feelings, and mood changes are common.

When people are immersed in a new culture, "culture shock" is a typical response. They should anticipate that they will probably feel bewildered and disoriented at times. This is normal when people neither speak the language nor understand the details of daily behavior. The newcomer may be unsure, for example, about when to shake hands or when to embrace. In some cases, it may even be difficult to know when a person means "yes" or "no".

After all, people can become overwhelmed when deprived of everything that was once familiar. The adult trying to become familiar with another culture may feel like a child. Stress, fatigue, and tension are common symptoms of culture shock.

Reactions to a new culture vary, but experience and research have shown that there are distinct stages in the adjustment process. Visitors coming for short periods do not always experience the same intense emotions as do immigrants from another country. A short-term adjustment for a one-year stay in a country could be represented by the following W-shaped diagram:

The "W" pattern of adjustment can also apply to longer stays (including permanent ones) in another culture. Each stage in the adjustment process is characterized by symptoms or outward signs typifying certain kinds of behavior:

1. Honeymoon period: Initially many people are fascinated and excited by everything in the new culture. The newcomer is elated to be experiencing a new culture. Interestingly, this level of elation may not be reached again.

2. Culture shock: The individuals are immersed in new problems: housing, transportation, employment, shopping, and language. Mental fatigue results from continuously straining to understand the new language and culture.

3. Initial adjustment: Everyday activities such as housing and shopping are no longer major

The "Re-entry Adjustment Process"

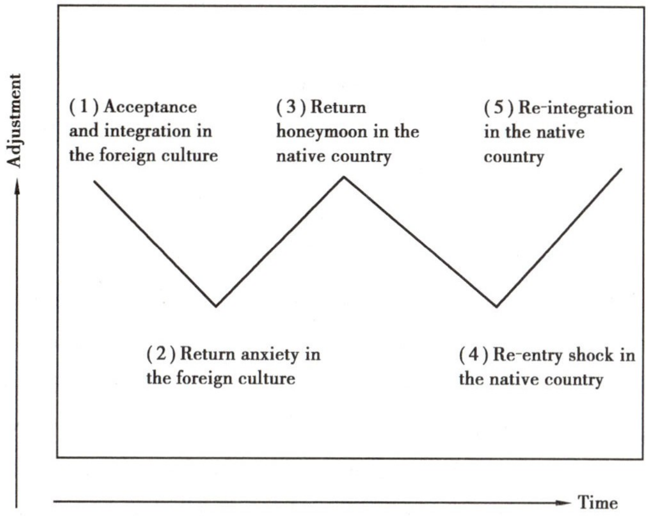

problems. The visitors may not yet be fluent in the spoken language, but they can now express their basic ideas and feelings.

4. Mental isolation: Individuals have been away from their family and good friends for a long time and may feel lonely. Many cannot express themselves as well as they could in their native language. Frustration and sometimes a loss of self-confidence result. Some individuals remain at this stage, particularly if they haven't been able to find a job.

5. Acceptance and integration: A routine (e.g., work, business, or school) has been established. The newcomers have become accustomed to the habits, customs, foods, and characteristics of the people in the new culture. They feel comfortable with friends, associates, and the language in the new country.

Individuals experience the stages of adjustment in different ways. Some people never experience a "honeymoon" period because the circumstances of their coming to a new country may have been too painful. In addition, certain stages last longer for some than for others, depending on such factors as the newcomer's personality, age, language and cultural competence, support from family and friends, financial situation, job status, and motivation for being in the new country.

Can a person accelerate or skip some of the more difficult stages of adjustment? Some people can, yet others cannot. This depends on individuals' ability to cope with changes in their life. Change is easier for some people than for others. Whenever people happen to be experiencing a negative stage of adjustment, they must be extremely patient and let time do its work.

How do people know that they are having problems adjusting to the new culture? Typical "symptoms" include the following:

1. Homesickness
2. Inability to work well
3. Too much eating, drinking, or sleeping

4. Anger toward the members of the new culture
5. Glorifying the native culture and emphasizing the negative in the new culture
6. Withdrawal and avoidance of contact with people from the new culture
7. Lack of ability to deal with even small problems

To a certain extent, all of these reactions are normal, and in a healthy adjustment, should be relatively short-term. When these responses last a long time or become exaggerated, the person may find it difficult to function on a daily basis. Note that the above list is not complete. The reader can probably think of more "symptoms".

One of the most important things a newcomer can do to facilitate adjustment is to try to develop social relationships with people from one's own country, with other newcomers, and with members of the new culture. It is essential to try to develop a group of friends with whom one can share new experiences. This is perhaps one of the fastest ways to begin to feel more at ease in another country.

Sometimes newcomers are eager to integrate and choose to give up their own culture. (Some people refer to this as "going native.") Others are fearful of cultural change and cling even more strongly to their own cultural traditions. Both giving up one's own culture and clinging to one's traditions may be extremities. Studies on cross-cultural adjustment suggest that maintaining a balance between two cultural patterns of behavior and beliefs can be helpful in the long term.

If newcomers try to become aware of cultural differences and make some modifications without attempting to change their basic personality, they will probably adjust fairly well to the new society. Newcomers can retain their individuality while becoming aware of differences. And, of course, some changes will have to be made. Feeling like a "fish out of water" shouldn't last forever.

(Adapted from Levine, D. R. and M. B. Adelman. 1993. *Beyond Language: Cross-cultural Communication*. 2nd ed. Englewood Cliffs, New Jersey: Prentice Hall Regents.)

Excercises

I. Multiple choices.

1. The phrase "a fish out of water" may refers to ________.
   A. a person poorly adapted to his or her own culture
   B. the reaction a person living in a new culture
   C. a person who is adjusting well to a new culture
2. A person who is adjusting to another culture typically ________.
   A. makes steady progress without having difficult times
   B. is continually depressed
   C. has "ups" and "downs"
3. The newness of a country can ________.
   A. be very interesting and motivating for the newcomer
   B. be bewildering and disorienting for the newcomer

C. Bother A and B.

4. What are common symptoms of culture shock?

A. Fatigue.

B. Tension.

C. Bother A and B.

5. In most people's experience in another culture, what usually takes place?

A. Total adjustment.

B. Partial adjustment.

C. No adjustment.

6. Of the six stages indicated on the graph, which is the most difficult?

A. Culture shock.

B. Mental isolation.

C. Honeymoon period.

7. Why might some people never experience a "honeymoon" stage?

A. They may have never been married.

B. They may have been forced to leave their country.

C. They might have to work immediately when they arrive.

8. Why do individuals have different rates of adjustment?

A. Because some people are extremely patient.

B. Because the ability to cope with change varies among individuals.

C. Because some people hate change.

9. Which of the followings are "symptoms" typical of adjustment difficulty?

A. Needing a lot of sleep; being unable to work well.

B. Criticizing the new culture.

C. Both A and B.

10. One of the fastest ways to begin to feel comfortable in another country is ________.

A. to develop a group of friends from your own country

B. to share your experiences with one or two individuals

C. to develop a group of friends including people from your own country, other newcomers, and members of the new society

II. The following are direct quotes from foreign people visiting or living in the United States. Based on the information in the reading, what stages in the cultural adjustment cycle are they experiencing?

1. "Frankly speaking, I do not feel that there are many pleasures for me in the United States right now. I am still seriously homesick, but I am getting better. I understand that this is the adjustment period. Hopefully, I will be back to normal soon. I think that when shock and frustration fade away, confidence and certainty of feeling will appear. I do believe that there are pleasures awaiting me."

Stage of adjustment: ______

2. "My feelings about living in a new country are quite complicated, but I can put them in one word: 'marvelous'. Everything seems wonderful and fresh to me. You can always learn something new every minute. And you can never tell what will happen the next minute."

   Stage of adjustment: ______

3. "When I arrived in this country I could only say 'thank you' and 'good-bye'. In spite of that, I had to get an apartment. My situation was really miserable because I couldn't understand what the managers were saying. They spoke so fast that I didn't understand anything, except 'OK?' or 'All right?' I almost started crying like a child on the street.

   Stage of adjustment: ______

III. Interview.

Here is a survey aiming to find out the degree of cultural shock. Find foreigners to fill up the form and write a study report. Share your study result with other groups.

Type of Cultural Shock	High Degree				Low Degree	None
1. Attitudes toward time	5	4	3	2	1	0
2. Attitudes toward women	5	4	3	2	1	0
3. Gestures, eye contact, and other nonverbal messages	5	4	3	2	1	0
4. Climate	5	4	3	2	1	0
5. Clothing/business dress	5	4	3	2	1	0
6. Customs, traditions, and beliefs	5	4	3	2	1	0
7. Educational system	5	4	3	2	1	0
8. Family and marriage practices	5	4	3	2	1	0
9. Financial problems	5	4	3	2	1	0
10. Food and diet	5	4	3	2	1	0
11. Housing	5	4	3	2	1	0
12. Lack of modern conveniences	5	4	3	2	1	0
13. Social class/Poverty/Wealth extremes	5	4	3	2	1	0
14. Social alienation (absence of people of same culture)	5	4	3	2	1	0
15. Standards of cleanliness	5	4	3	2	1	0
16. Transportation	5	4	3	2	1	0

Continued

Type of Cultural Shock	High Degree				Low Degree	None
17. Values and ethical standards	5	4	3	2	1	0
18. Work habits and practices	5	4	3	2	1	0

Movie Theatre

Outsourced is a romantic comedy film, directed by John Jeffcoat, released in 2006.

This film is about an American expatriate manager, Todd Anderson (Josh Hamilton) who has to travel to India to train his Indian employees. Going through a disastrous period of cultural conflicts, Todd finally started to appreciate the Indian culture and is getting used to new working environment.

Watch this movie and pick up all the cultural shock Mr. Todd encountered in Indian.

UNIT 6 Time and Culture

Pre-class Activity

When Should I Be There?

Discuss the following questions.

1. Your American friend invited you to her party tonight at 7:30. When are you supposed to get there? Why?

   A. Before 7:00, to help her to prepare.

   B. 5 to 10 minutes late, not to be the first guest.

   C. After 8:00. I'm the VIP.

   D. 5 to 10 minutes earlier. It is a polite way to show my respect for her.

   How about in China?

2. Your American friend invited you to her house for dinner at 6:30. When are you supposed to get there?

   A. Right on time.

   B. Be fashionably late.

   C. Half an hour late.

   D. About 5 to 10 minutes earlier.

   How about in China?

Read to Learn More

Text

Time

Three centuries ago, when the Dutch mathematician Christian Hygens built the first pendulum clock, which allowed people to keep track of hours and minutes, little did he know how much impact his invention would have on people's lives. You now strap clocks to your wrists, hang them on your walls, see them on your computer screen, and give them power to control everything from your moods to your relationships. Anthropologists Rapport and Overing underscore the importance of time to human behavior when they wrote, "to cut up life into moments of being, in sum, is for the individual to possess means by which that life can be filled, shaped and reshaped in significant ways." Self-reflection will reveal how time communicates. If you arrive thirty minutes late for an important appointment and offer no apology, you send a certain message about yourself. Telling someone how guilty you feel about your belated arrival also sends a message. Studies even point out that one of the hallmarks of a successful and intimate relationship is the amount of time people spend together. What is happening is obvious; how the parties are perceiving and using time is sending a message about how much they are for each other. Of course, there is much more to time than what it says about your relationships. Gonzales and Zimbardo accentuate this multidimensional aspect of time when they wrote, "Our temporal perspective influences a wide range of psychological processes, from motivation, emotion and spontaneity to risk taking, creativity and problem-solving." Your own experience tells you that in North America, most members of the dominant culture adhere to the advice of Benjamin Franklin that tells them "time is money". Think of what is being said about the use of time in the common expressions "he who hesitates is lost" and "just give me the bottom line".

As is in the case with all aspects of nonverbal communication, culture plays a substantial role in how you perceive and use time. As Lewis points out, "fatalism, work ethic, reincarnation, *susu*, Confucianism, *Weltschmerz*, *dusha*, etc., all reveal different motions about time." Ballard and Seibold establish much the same link between culture and time when they note: "the existence and proliferation of objective, independent time-measuring devices is itself a cultural by-product, and the uniform seconds, minutes, and hours that clocks appear to 'measure' also are culturally constructed." Gannon highlights the bond between time and culture in the United States when he writes:

> *Time is also limited in America because there are so many things to do in one's lifetime. The society develops technologically at horrendous speed, and it's difficult to keep up. One has to be continuously on the move. This is American: there is little time for contemplating or meditating.*

As you would suspect, when cultures use time in dissimilar ways, problems can occur. As Novinger states, "when people of two different cultures 'use' time differently, their interaction can generate misunderstanding, misinterpretation, and ill will." A culture's conception of time can be examined from three different perspectives: (1) *informal time*; (2) *perceptions of past, present, and future*; and (3) *Hall's monochronic and polychromic classifications.*

Informal Time

Punctuality. In most instances, rules for informal time, such as punctuality and pace, are not explicitly taught. Like most of culture, these rules usually function below the level of consciousness. Argyle makes much the same point when he compares cultural differences in punctuality standards:

> *How late is "late"? This varies greatly. In Britain and America one may be 5 minutes late for a business appointment, but not 15 and certainly not 30 minutes late, which is perfectly normal in Arab countries. On the other hand, in Britain it is correct to be 5 to 15 minutes late for an invitation to dinner. An Italian might arrive 2 hours late, an Ethiopian after, and Japanese not at all—he had accepted only to prevent his host from losing face.*

As the above example demonstrates, reaction to punctuality is rooted in our cultural experiences. In the United States, you have all learned that the boss can arrive late for a meeting without anyone raising an eyebrow; if the secretary is late, he or she may receive a reprimand in the form of a stern glance. A rock star or a physician can keep people waiting for long periods of time, but the warm-up band and the food caterer had better be on time. In Latin America, one is expected to arrive late to appointments as a sign of respect. In fact, in Chile it is even considered rude to be on time to social events. This same notion of time is seen in Spain, where, according to Lewis, there is the belief that "punctuality messes up schedules". In Africa, people often "show up late for appointments, meetings, and social engagements". There is even a Nigerian expression that says, "a watch did not invent man." These two views of tardiness would be perceived as rudeness in Germany. According to Hall and Hall, "Promptness is taken for granted in Germany—in fact, it's almost an obsession."

Pace. We can determine a culture's attitude toward time by examining the pace at which members of that culture perform specific acts. Americans, because of the pace of life in the United States, always seem to be in a hurry. As Kim observes, "life is in constant motion. People consider time to be wasted or lost unless they are doing something." Conveniences help—from fast-food restaurants to one-stop gas stations to microwave ovens—as Andersen and Wang point out, "in the United States, time is viewed as a commodity that can be wasted, spent, saved, and used wisely." The attitude toward time means that Americans want to get things done quickly. Americans are constantly seeking faster computers and cars. People in the United States grow up hearing others tell them not "to waste so much time" and "actions speak louder than words". Other cultures see time differently and hence live lives at a pace different from that of most people in the United States. Asselin and Mastron point out that "the French do not share the American sense of urgency to accomplish tasks. The Japanese and Chinese cultures also treat time in ways that often appear at cross purposes with American goals. The Chinese have a proverb that states, "he who hurries cannot walk with dignity." Drawing on the Japanese culture for his example, Brislin illustrates how pace is reflected in the negotiation process:

> *When negotiating with the Japanese, Americans like to get right down to business. They were socialized to believe that "time is money". They can accept about 15 minutes of "small talk" about the weather, their trip, and baseball, but more than that becomes unreasonable. The Japanese, on the other hand, want to get to know their business counterparts. They feel that the best way to do this is to have long conversations with Americans about a wide variety of topic. The Japanese are comfortable with hours and hours, and even days and days, of conversation.*

Indonesians are yet another group that does not hurry. They perceive time as a limitless pool. According to Harris and Moran, there is even "a phrase in Indonesia describing this concept that translates as 'rubber time', so that time stretches or shrinks and it is therefore very flexible." People in Latin America also have a view of time that sees them conducting their business at a slower pace than the one found in the United States. For these cultures there is a belief that "there is always another day". In Africa, where a slow pace is the rule, "people who rush are suspected of trying to cheat," says Ruch.

As we have mentioned elsewhere, nonverbal behavior is often directly linked to a culture's religious and value orientation. This notion is made manifest when you turn to the Arab culture. When we look at Islam, most Arabs believe that their destiny is a matter of fate. The Arab connection to the pace of life and time is clearly pointed out by Abu-Gharbieh:

> *Throughout the Arab world, there is nonchalance about time and deadlines: the pace of life is more leisurely than that in the West. Social events and appointments tend not to have fixed beginning or end.*

Manifestations of pace assume a host of forms. One study, for example, pointed out that even the speed at which people walk reflects a culture's concept of time. People from England and the United States move much faster than people from Indonesia.

Past, Present, and Future

Past Orientation. As the word "past" tells you, cultures with this orientation attach great importance to the past and see what went before as a gauge for their current perception of people and events. Richmond, McCracken, and Paye offer an excellent summary of the link between the past and comprehending the present: "cultures that have a past-oriented philosophy tend to apply past events to similar new situations. These societies have respect for the elderly and listen to what their senior citizens have to say regarding the past." As we mentioned, knowing that a culture is past oriented can give you insight into how members of that culture view the world and other people. For example, the British place much emphasis on tradition and are often perceived as resisting change. A statement often heard in England when people ask about the monarchy is "we have always done it this way." The Chinese and Japanese, with their traditions of ancestor worship and strong pride in their cultures' persistence for thousands of years, are also cultures that use the past as a guide to how to live in the present. As a Chinese proverb advises, "consider the past and you will know the present." The Irish and Irish Americans also take great pride in their past, making them yet another culture that is past oriented. As Wilson notes, "Irish-Americans, with their strong sense of tradition, are typically past oriented. They have an allegiance to the past, their ancestors, and their history. The past is often the focus of Irish stories."

American Indians represent another culture that uses the past to help explain and understand life. Still and Hodgins explain this approach in the following manner:

> *Most American Indian tribes are not future oriented. Very little planning is done for the future because their view is that many things are outside of the individual's control and may affect or change the future. In fact, the Navajo language does not include a future tense verb. Time is not viewed as a constant or something that one can control, but rather as something that is always with the individual. Thus, to plan for the future is something viewed as foolish.*

Present Orientation. In this orientation, the past is not nearly as important as the present. Present-oriented people see the future as ambiguous and capricious. Filipinos and Latin Americans are cultures that emphasize enjoying and living in the moment. These cultures tend to be more impulsive and spontaneous than others and often have a casual, relaxed lifestyle. Mexican Americans also have a culture that "tends to focus on the present and a more flexible attitude toward time". Because of this outlook, "the quality of an interpersonal relationship, rather than the amount of time spent with someone, is of higher importance." This approach to time frequently misinterprets a concern with the present as a sign of indolence and inefficiency.

Future Orientation. In future-oriented cultures, what is yet to come is most valued. Change, taking chances, and optimism are part of the hallmarks of cultures that hold to this orientation. This view toward the future is the one most Americans have. As a people, Americans are constantly planning for the future, and their children play with toys (dolls, cars, guns, and so on) that prepare them for adulthood. Many of you can hardly wait to finish what you are doing so that you can move on to something else. As we noted during our discussion of pace, having an eye to the future often produces a very low tolerance for extensions and postponements. What you want, you want now, so you can dispose of this moment and move on to the next. In addition, future-oriented cultures welcome innovation and "have less regard for past social or organizational customs and traditions."

Distinctions in time orientations, like all aspects of nonverbal communication, can create communication differences. A business meeting involving these three orientations might look something like the following conversations:

Past orientation: Why don't we look at how much success we had with a similar merger with a Japanese company five years ago?

Present orientation: Just wait a second. It really doesn't matter what we did five years ago. The key is what we want to do now.

Future orientation: Only worrying about what is going on now is shortsighted. For this company to make money we need to think about what this merger will mean in the future.

Monochronic (M-time) and Polychronic (P-time) Classifications

Anthropologist Edward T. Hall advanced another classification of time as a form of communication. Hall proposed that cultures organize time in one of two ways: either monochronic (M-time) or polychronic (P-time). Hall's classifications represent two distinct approaches to perceiving and utilizing time.

M-time. As the word monochronic implies, this concept explains time as lineal and segmented. More specifically, "A monochronic view of time believes time is a scarce resource which must be rationed and controlled through the use of schedules and appointments, and through aiming to do only one thing at any one time." Novinger sums up the characteristics of monochronic cultures by noting, "cultures that are monochronic have a predominantly linear and sequential approach to time that is rational, suppresses spontaneity and tends to focus on one activity at a time." Cultures with this orientation would, of course, value punctuality, good organization, and the judicious use of time. The English naturalist Charles Darwin abstracted this view of time when he wrote, "A man who dares to waste one hour of time has not discovered the value of life." The time clock records the hours you must work, the school bell moves you from class to class, and the calendar marks important days and events in your lives.

Cultures that can be classified as M-time are people from Germany, Austria, Switzerland, and America. As Hall explains, "People of the Western world, particularly Americans, tend to think of time as something fixed in nature, something around us and from which we cannot escape; an ever-present part of the environment, just like the air we breathe." According to Trompenaars and Hampden-Turner, you can see in the business setting how cultures that view time in a sequential pattern would schedule in advance and not run late and have "a strong preference for following initial plans".

P-time. People from cultures on polychromic time live their lives quite differently than do those who move to the monochronic clock. People and human relationships are at the center of polychromic cultures. As Smith and Bond point out, "a polychromic view of time sees the maintenance of harmonious relationships as the important agenda, so that use of time needs to be flexible in order that we do right by various people to whom we have obligations." These cultures are normally collective and deal with life in a holistic manner. For P-time cultures, time is less tangible; hence, feelings of wasted time are not as prevalent as in M-time cultures. They can interact with more than one person or do more than one thing at a time. Gannon offers an excellent example of the multidimensional nature of P-time when he talks of the Turkish culture. "'Polychronism' best describes the Turkish ability to concentrate on different things simultaneously at work, at home, or in the coffee house." Because P-time suggests this notion of multiple activities and flexibility, Dresser believes it "explains why there is more interrupting in conversations carried on by people from Arabic, Asian, and Latin American cultures." Africans are yet another culture that takes great stock in the activity that is occurring at the moment and emphasize people more than schedules. As Richmond and Gestrin note, "time for Africans is defined by events rather than the clock or calendar." "For Africans, the person they are with is more important than the one who is out of sight." This leads, of course, to a lifestyle that to outsiders appears to be spontaneous and unstructured.

Within the United States, there are co-cultures that use time differently from the dominant culture. Mexican Americans frequently speak of "Latino time" when their timing varies from that of the dominant culture. Burgoon and Saine have observed that the Polynesian culture of Hawaii has "Hawaiian time", a concept of time that is very relaxed and reflects the informal lifestyle of the native Hawaiian people. And among Samoans, there is a time perspective referred to as "coconut time", which is derived from the notion that it is not necessary to pick coconuts because they will fall when the time is right. African Americans often use what is referred to as "BPT" (Black People's Time) or "hang-loose time". This concept, which has its roots in the P-time cultures of Africa, maintains that priority belongs to what is happening at that instant. Statements such as "Hey, man, what's happening?" reflect the importance of the here and now. In the table below, Hall and Hall summarize the basic aspects of monochronic and polichronic time. Their condensation takes many of the ideas we have mentioned and translates them into specific behaviors.

Comparison of Monochronic and Polychronic Cultures

Monochronic Time People	Polychronic Time People
Do one thing at a time	Do many things at once
Concentrate on the job	Are easily distracted and subject to interruption
Take time commitments (deadlines, schedules) seriously	Consider time commitments an objective to be achieved, if possible
Are low context and need information	Are high context and already have information
Are committed to the job	Are committed to people and human relationships
Adhere to plans	Change plans often and easily
Are concerned about not disturbing others; follow rules of privacy	Are more concerned with people close to them (family, friends, close business associates) than with privacy

Continued

Monochronic Time People	Polychronic Time People
Show great respect for private property; seldom borrow or lend	Borrow and lend things often and easily
Emphasize promptness	Base promptness on the relationship
Are accustomed to short-term relationships	Have strong tendency to build lifetime relationships

(Adapted from: Hall E. T. and M. R. Hall. 1990. *Understanding Cultural Differences: Germans, French and Americans*. Yarmouth, ME: Intercultural Press, p. 15.

Samovar, L. A., R. E. Porter, & E.R. McDaniel. 2009. *Communication Between Cultures*. 6th ed. Beijing: Peking University Press, pp. 219-24.)

After reading activity

1. ***How late can you be for the following in your own culture?***

   a) a class

   b) work

   c) a job interview

   d) a dinner party

   e) a date with a friend

   Now ask these questions of members of people from other cultures.

2. ***Find information from the text to fill in the table below.***

Time Orientation	Definition	Characteristics	Countries
Past			
Present			
Future			

3. ***Are you a Polychronic Person or a Monochronic Person?***

   The scale is designed to measure one's polychronic and/or monochronic time orientation.

   Scores of approximately 30 and below indicate a monochrome orientation.

   Scores of approximately 42 and above indicate a polychrome orientation.

   Scale: 1—strongly agree, 2—agree, 3—neutral, 4—disagree, 5—strongly disagree

   (1) ____ I usually feel frustrated after I choose to do a number of tasks when I could have chosen to do one at a time.

   (2) ____ When I talk with my friends in a group setting, I feel comfortable trying to hold two or three conversations at a time.

(3) ____ When I work on a project around the house, it doesn't bother me to stop in the middle of one job to pick up another job that needs to be done.

(4) ____ I like to finish one task before going on to another task.

(5) ____ At church it wouldn't bother me to meet at the same time with several different people who all had different church matters to discuss.

(6) ____ I tend to concentrate on one job before moving on to another task.

(7) ____ The easiest way for me to function is to organize my day with activities with a schedule.

(8) ____ If I were a teacher and had several students wishing to talk with me about the assigned homework, I would meet with the whole group rather than one student at a time.

(9) ____ I like doing several tasks at one time.

(10) ____ I am frustrated when I have to start on a task without first finishing a previous one.

(11) ____ In trying to solve problems, I find it stimulating to think about several different problems at the same time.

Kaleidoscope

Time-use Patterns in Nonofficial Chinese Contexts

There are a number of differences between Chinese and Westerners in their use of time in nonofficial contexts. One of your first big surprises is likely to occur when a Chinese visitor arrives early. Not two or three minutes early, but fifteen or more minutes early. The situation can be quite awkward, particularly if you are still getting prepared. What do you do, for example, when you've come out of the bath with only a towel to shout, "Who is it?" through the door? You may have no option but to leave your visitor shuffling around in the hallway while you get dressed. To avoid this you could tell your first-time guests the usual practice in the West before they come.

The Chinese, if asked, might suggest that they arrive so early because they do not wish to waste the host's time. (Apparent logic here is that if the meeting can be completed before the time it was scheduled to begin, then none of the host's time has been wasted.) Our view, however, is that their motive for arriving early is to demonstrate deep respect for the host, who at this point is invariably someone with whom they are not well acquainted. As the relationship grows warmer over subsequent days and weeks, the Chinese arrive less and less early until, finally, they settle into their standard pattern: arriving more or less on time.

The nature of traditional visiting practices may help to explain why the Chinese are less aware than Westerners of the difficulties potentially caused by very early arrivals. Among farmers and other Chinese connected with agriculture, no prior arrangement is thought necessary for any kind of gathering of friends or family members. In the countryside, one may arrive at a friend's home without prior notice and enter without waiting to be admitted. Regardless of whether one wishes to see a friend to discuss a specific issue or merely to kill the time, one simply walks in, perhaps calling out the name of the person being sought. Homes are open to their owners' friends all the time. The concept of privacy as we understand it in individualistic Western cultures does not exist in the traditional collectivist culture of China.

With the dramatic increase of home phones and cellular phones in the cities, unannounced visiting has become less common. Educators, scientists, technicians, and people in similar professions schedule their time carefully; to Chinese as well as Western businesspeople and managers, "time is money." Although dropping in to someone's office just to say hello is still possible, the general rule is that if you wish to see someone on business, prior arrangement is necessary. (Even before they visit each other, neighbors in large cities usually phone first to make sure that they will be welcome.)

Regardless of these gradual changes, the norm still prevails that anyone may visit a very close friend at his or her office without prior notice at almost any time. Visitors need wait outside only if strangers are already inside.

Some Chinese families in urban areas are developing guidelines regarding the times when they prefer to receive visitors in their homes. For example, some families may say that you are welcome to visit during Saturday afternoon or at any time on Sunday. There are genuine open hours: still, there are restrictions to keep in mind. Unless you are on exceptionally friendly terms, you should not arrive during early afternnon or at suppertime. In China, noon to 13:00 is the time for lunch, and 13:00 to 14:00 (in winter) or 14:30 (in summer) is the time for *wushui*, the afternoon nap. Although the tradition of *wushui* is gradually declining in Beijing and other major urban areas, and young people do not normally nap now, it continues to be quite prevalent among the Chinese in other parts of China, especially in its southern provinces.

Supper is usually eaten between 18:00 and 19:00. (These times might be slightly earlier during the winter and slightly later during the summer.) You should never arrive earlier than 9:00 or later than 20:00.

Because of your cultural conditioning, it may be difficult for you to fully adopt the traditional Chinese habit of showing up for a visit without any prior knowledge of the host's preferences regarding impromptu visits. But if you do come to feel comfortable enough to attempt unannounced visiting of Chinese friends, keep the following in mind: if you unexpectedly come into a household immediately before or during a meal, you will likely be invited to join the family at table. This invitation, though polite, is probably not genuine, so you should decline it and depart unless a truly energetic and convincing effort is made to persuade you to remain.

For Westerners, visiting Chinese friends is not likely to require major adjustments. Since you are culturally conditioned to make appointments for all types of visits and to be punctual, you are not likely to cause annoyance or misunderstanding by showing up at the wrong time. If there is any danger, it is that you will unnecessarily isolate yourself from your Chinese friends by feeling reluctant to visit them without having a definite invitation.

(Source: Adapted from Hu Wenzhong, Cornelius N. Grove, and Zhuang Enping. 2010.

Encountering the Chinese: A Modern Country, An Ancient Culture. 3rd ed. Boston/London: Intercultural Press. pp: 32-34.)

Mini-case Study

U.S. Professor in Brazil

I accepted an appointment as visiting professor of psychology at the federal university in Niterio, Brazil, a mid-sized city across the bay from Rio de Janeiro. As I left home for my first day of class, I asked someone the time. It was 9:05 a.m. which allowed me time to relax and look around the campus before my 10 o'clock lecture. After what I judged to be half an hour, I glanced at a clock I was passing. It said 10:20! In panic, I broke for the classroom followed by gentle calls of "Hola, professor" and "Tudobem, professor" from unhurried students, many of whom, I later realized, were my own. I arrived breathless to find an empty room.

Frantically, I asked a passerby the time. "9:45" was the answer. No, that couldn't be. I asked someone else. "9:45." Another said "exactly 9:43." The clock in a nearby office read 3:15. I had learned my first lesson about Brazilians: their timepieces are consistently inaccurate. And nobody minds.

My class was scheduled from 10 until noon. Many students came late, some very late. Several arrived after 10:30.A few showed up close to 11. Two came after that. All of the latercomers wore relaxed smiles. Each one said hello, and although a few apologized briefly, none seemed terribly concerned about lateness. They assumed that I understood. The idea of Brazilians arriving late was not a great shock... the real surprise came at noon that first day, when the end of class arrived.

Back home in California, I never need to look at a clock to know when the class hour is ending, the shuffling of books is accompanied by strained expressions. When noon arrived in my first Brazilian class, only a few students left immediately. Others slowly drifted out during the next 15 minutes, and some continued asking me questions long after that.

Questions

1. Why did the Professor panic when he saw the time indicated on a clock he just passed by?
2. Was the Professor late for his class?
3. Why do Brazilians not care about the accuracy of their clocks?
4. Can the Professor know the time when the class hour is ending without looking at the clock or watch in Brazil?
5. What kind of the time-oriented culture do Americans and Brazilians belong to respectively?

After-class Exercises

Reading

Time

For Americans, time is a resource that, like water or coal, can be used well or poorly. "Time is money," they say. "You only get so much time in this life; you'd best use it wisely." As Americans are trained to see things, the future will not be better than the past or the present unless people use their time for constructive, future-oriented activities. Thus, Americans admire a "well-organized" person, one who has a list of things to do—either on a piece of paper or in a personal digital assistant—and a schedule for doing them. The ideal person is punctual (that is, arrives at the scheduled time for a meeting or event) and is considerate of other people's time (that is, does not "waste people's time" with conversation or other activity that has no visible, beneficial outcome).

Early in his long and productive career, American anthropologist Edward T. Hall lived and worked on reservations belonging to two native American Indian groups, the Navajo and the Hopi. He discovered that the Native American's notion of time was very different from the one he learned growing up as a European American man. In describing his experience on the reservation, Hall later wrote,

During my five-year stay on the reservations, I found that, in general, the Indians believed that whites were crazy, although they didn't tell us that. We were always hurrying to get someplace when that place would still be there whenever we arrived. Whites had a kind of devil inside who seemed to drive them unmercifully. That devil's name was Time. ①

The American attitude toward time is not necessarily shared by others, especially non-Europeans. Most people on our planet are more likely to conceive of time as something that is simply there, around them, not something to "use". One of the more difficult things many international businesspeople and students in the United States must adjust to is the notion that time must be saved whenever possible and used wisely every day.

In their efforts to use their time wisely, Americans are sometimes seen by international visitors as automatons, inhuman creatures who are so tied to their clocks, their schedules, and their daily plans that they cannot participate in or enjoy the human interactions that are necessary to a fulfilling life. "They are like little machines running around," one international visitor said.

The premium Americans place on efficiency is closely related to their concepts of the future,

---

① Hall, Edward T. 1992. *An Anthropology of Everyday Life*. New York: Anchor/Doubleda.

change, and time. To do something efficiently is to do it in the way that is quickest and requires the smallest expenditure of resources. This may be why e-mail and text messages have become such popular means of communication in American society. Students commonly correspond with their professors by e-mail or text message rather than waiting to talk with them during their office hours. Likewise, businesspeople frequently check their electronic mail not just while on the job but also before and after work, on weekends, and even while on vacation. Popular magazines offer suggestions for more efficient ways to shop, cook, clean house, do errands, raise children, tend the yard, and on and on. The Internet provides immediate access to all kinds of information and products. Americans have come to expect instant responses to phone calls, e-mails, text messages, faxes, and other forms of communication. Many quickly become impatient if the responses aren't immediate, even when there is no apparent urgency.

In this context the "fast-food industry" is an excellent example of an American cultural product. McDonald's, KFC, Pizza Hut, and other fast-food establishments prosper in a country where many people want to minimize the amount of time spent preparing and eating meals. The millions of Americans who take their meals at fast-food restaurants cannot be interested in lingering over their food while talking with friends, in the way millions of Europeans do. As McDonald's restaurants have spread around the world, they have come to symbolize American culture, bringing not just hamburgers but an emphasis on speed, efficiency, and shiny cleanliness. The typical American food, some observers argue, is fast food.

Also in this context, it will surprise many visitors form Europe or Japan to see that some of the newer electronic communications devices commonly used in their countries, such as wands to pay for purchases, are not widespread in the United States. Their admiration for technology and efficiency does not necessarily mean that Americans always have the most advanced technological devices at their disposal.

(Source: Althen, Gary & Janet Bennett. 2010. *American Ways—A Cultural Guide to the United States*. 3rd Edition. Boston/London: Intercultural Press, pp.19-21.)

Excercises

1. ***Look for words or phrases from the text to fill in the blanks.***

   1) Americans see time as ______________________________

   2) For Americans, time should be used for constructive and ______________ activities.

   3) Americans admire people who are ____________, ____________ and considerate of other people's time.

   4) Other cultures often consider time as ______________________________.

   5) Americans are expected to do things in a high ____________ way. They easily get impatient if the responses aren't ____________.

2. ***Translate the following phrases into English.***

1）消磨时间；节省时间；浪费时间；争取时间；花时间在……

2）停止不前；跟上潮流

3）岁月不等人；一寸光阴一寸金

3. ***Discussion.***

1）How does Americans' conception of time affect their life and work？

2）Do you think the development of science and the ability of innovation are closely to a future-oriented culture？

UNIT 7 Verbal Communication: The Way People Speak

Pre-class Activity

Responses to the Same Situation

People from different cultures speak in different ways. The following questions are intended to help you find proper responses in the area of verbal communication in the context of American culture. First, write an answer that describes a likely response in your country. On the multiple-choice questions, try to guess what an American would say and do. More than one answer may be correct.

1. When someone compliments the dress you are wearing, you would:

   In your country: ______________________

   In the United States:

   A. Say, "Oh this cheap thing? It's not worth much."

   B. Give it to him.

   C. Say, "Thanks," and smile.

   D. Say, "would you like to have it?"

2. It is not considered appropriate to give compliments to:

   In your country: ______________________

   In the United States:

   A. A woman about her husband.

   B. A man about his wife.

   C. A couple about their child.

   D. A doctor about his or her salary.

3. To which of the following statements would you respond "thank you"?

   In your country: ______________________

   In the United States:

   A. "You are a clever person."

   B. "Let me open the door for you."

   C. "Your have a beautiful face."

D. "Please accept this gift as a symbol of our friendship."

4. Someone who wanted to criticize the behavior of a fellow student would:

In your country: ____________________

In the United States:

A. Say something to the student in front of the class.

B. Tell the teacher to speak to the student.

C. Speak to the student after class.

5. If students want to criticize the way a professor teaches, they should:

In your country: ____________________

In the United States:

A. Go directly to the dean of the department.

B. Ask the professor for an appointment to talk about the class.

C. Go directly to the professor's office with several other students and state the complaint.

D. Complain to the professor during class time.

6. What would be a polite way to evade a question that you don't want to answer (e.g., "What do you think of the government in your country?")

In your country: ____________________

In the United States:

A. "It's none of your business."

B. "I refuse to answer that question."

C. "That question is inappropriate, so I can't answer it."

D. "Oh, I don't know. I'm not very interested in politics."

7. If someone uses a foreign word or phrase you don't know, you might:

In your country: ____________________

In the United States:

A. Say, "Please repeat."

B. Say, "I'm sorry, I didn't understand what you said. Could you please repeat that last sentence (or word)?"

C. Say nothing and pretend that you have understood.

D. Say, "Excuse me, but what does that sentence (or word) mean?"

8. If someone offers you food that you really don't like, you might say:

In your country: ____________________

In the United States:

A. "I hate that."

B. "Sure, I'd love some more."

C. "I'll have just a little bit, please."

D. "Thanks, but I'm really full."

9. Which topics are inappropriate to discuss immediately after an introduction?

In your country: ____________________

In the United States:

A. Marital status.

B. Religion.

C. Age.

D. Occupation.

Read to Learn More

Text

(1)

The Sapir-Whorf Hypothesis of Linguistic Relativity

Every language has its unique features and ways of allowing those who speak it to identify specific objects and experiences. These linguistic features, which distinguish each language from all other, affect how the speakers of the language perceive and experience the world. Although many scholars have advanced ideas and theories about the relationships among language, thought, culture, and intercultural communication, the names most often associated with these issues are Benjamin Lee Whorf and Edward Sapir. Their theory is called linguistic relativity.

Until the early part of the twentieth century, in Western Europe and the United States, language was generally assumed to be a neutral medium that did not influence the way people experienced the world. During that time, the answer to the preceding question would have been that, regardless of whether people grew up learning and speaking Arabic or Tagalog, they would experience the world similarly. The varying qualities of language would not have been expected to affect the people who spoke those languages. Language, from this point of view, was merely a vehicle by which ideas were presented, rather than a shaper of the very substance of those ideas.

In 1921, anthropologist Edward Sapir began to articulate an alternative view of language, asserting that language influenced or even determined the ways in which people thought. Sapir's students, Benjamin Whorf, continued to develop Sapir's ideas through the 1940s. Together, their ideas became subsumed under several labels, including the theory of linguistic determinism, the theory of linguistic relativity, the Sapir-Whorf hypothesis, and the Whorfian hypothesis. The following quotation from Sapir is typical of their statements:

> *Human beings do not live in the objective world alone, nor alone in the world of social activity as ordinarily understood, but are very much at the mercy of the particular language which has become the medium of expression for their society. It is quite an illusion to imagine that one adjusts to reality essentially without the use of language and that language is merely an incidental means of solving specific problems of communication or reflection. The*

fact of the matter is that the "real world" is to a large extent unconsciously built up on the language habits of the group... The worlds in which different societies (cultures) live are distinct worlds, not merely the same world with different labels attached... We see and hear and otherwise experience very largely as we do because the language habits of our community predispose certain choices of interpretation.

Our discussion of the Sapir-Whorf hypothesis is not intended to provide a precise rendering as articulated by Sapir and Whorf, which is virtually impossible to do. During the twenty years in which they formally presented their ideas to the scholarly community, their views shifted somewhat, and their writings include both "firmer", or more deterministic views of the relationship between language and thought, and "soft" views that describe language as merely influencing or shaping thought.

In the "firm", or deterministic, version of the people learning a language, they are irrevocably affected by its particulars. Furthermore, it is never possible to translate effectively and successfully between languages, which makes competent intercultural communication an elusive goal.

The "soft" position is a less causal view of the nature of the language-thought relationship. In this version, language shapes how people think and experience their world, but his influence is not unceasing. Instead, it is possible for people from different initial language systems to learn words and categories sufficiently similar to their own so that communication can be accurate.

If substantial evidence had been found to support the firm version of the Sapir-Whorf hypothesis, it would represent a dismal prognosis for competent intercultural communication. Because so few people grow up bilingually, it would be impossible to transcend the boundaries of their linguistic experiences. Fortunately, the weight of the scholarly evidence, which we summarize in the following section, debunks the notion that people's first language traps them inescapably in a particular pattern of thinking. Instead, evidence suggests that language plays a powerful role in *shaping* how people think and experience the world. Although the shaping properties of language are significant, linguistic equivalence can be established between people from different language systems.

Sapir and Whorf's major contribution to the study of intercultural communication is that they called attention to the integral relationship among thought, culture, and language.

(Adapted from Lustig, M. W. & J. Koester. 2010. *Intercultural Competence: Interpersonal Communication Across Cultures. 6th Edition.* Boston: Pearson, pp. 177-179.)

After reading activity

1. ***Discussion.***

1) Why is Sapir and Whorf's work called "hypothesis"? What is the positive contribution made by their research and what is its defect?

2) Do you believe it is the language we speak that SHAPES the world we know?

3) What kinds of family relationships in each culture can be perceived from the English kinship terms and their Chinese counterparts? Examples as following:

English	Chinese
Father	父亲
Mother	母亲
brother	兄、弟
sister	姐、妹
Father-in-law	家翁、岳父
Mother-in-law	家婆、岳母
uncle	叔、伯
aunt	姨、姑
cousin	堂、表兄弟姐妹
…	……

2. ***According to the Sapir-Whorf hypothesis, it might be a mission-impossible trying to do a perfect translation from one language to another. Do you support this claim or not? Use examples to illustrate your points.***

(2)
Context and Meaning

One of the functions of culture is to provide a highly selective screen between man and the outside world. In its many forms, culture therefore designates what we pay attention to and what we ignore. This screening function provides structure for the world and protects the nervous system from "information overload". Information overload is a technical term applied to information-processing systems. It describes a situation in which the system breaks down when it cannot properly handle the huge volume of information to which it is subjected. Any mother who is trying to cope with the demands of small children, run a house, enjoy her husband, and carry on even a modest social life knows that there are times when everything happens at once and the world seems to be closing in on her. She is experiencing the same information overload that afflicts business managers, administrators, physicians, attorneys, and air controllers. Institutions such as stock exchanges, libraries, and telephone systems also go through times when the demands on the system (inputs) exceed capacity.

People can handle the crunch through delegating and establishing priorities; while institutional solutions are less obvious, the high-context rule seems to apply. That is, the only way to increase information-handling capacity without increasing the mass and complexity of the system is to program the memory of the system so that less information is required to activate the system, i.e., make it more like the couple that has been married for thirty-five years. The solution to the problem of coping with increased complexity and greater demands on the system seems to lie in the preprogramming of the individual or organization. This is done by means of the "contexting" process.

The importance of the role of context is widely recognized in the communication fields, yet the process is rarely described adequately, or if it is, the insights gained are not acted upon. Before dealing with context as a way of handling information overload, let me describe how I envisage the contexting process, which is an emergent function; i.e., we are just discovering what it is and how it works. Closely related to the high-low-context continuum is the degree to which one is aware of the selective screen that when one moves from the low to the high side of the scale, awareness of the selective process increases. Therefore, what one pays attention to, context, and information overload are all functionally related.

In the fifties, the United Sates Government spent millions of dollars developing systems for machine translation of Russian and other languages. After years of effort on the part of some of the most talented linguists in the country, it was finally concluded that the only reliable, and ultimately the fastest, translator is a human being deeply conversant not only with the language but with the subject as well. The computers could spew out yards of print-out but they meant very little. The words and some of the grammar were all there, but the sense was distorted. That the project failed was not due to lack of application, time, money, or talent, but for other reasons, which are central to the theme of this unit.

The problem lies not in the linguistic code but in the context, which carries varying proportions of the meaning. Without context, the code is incomplete since it encompasses only part of the message. This should become clear if one remembers that the spoken language is an abstraction of an event that happened, might have happened, or is being planned. As any writer knows, an event is usually infinitely more complex and rich than the language used to describe it. Moreover, the writing system is an abstraction of the spoken system and is in effect reminder system of what somebody said or could have said. In the process of abstracting, as contrasted with measuring, people take in some things and unconsciously ignore others. This is what intelligence is: paying attention to the right things. The linear quality of a language inevitably results in accentuating some things at the expense of others. Two languages provide interesting contrasts. In English, when a man says, "It rained last night," there is no way of knowing how he arrived at that conclusion, or if he is even telling the truth, whereas a Hopi cannot talk about the rain at all without signifying the nature of his relatedness to the event—firsthand experience, inference, or hearsay. This is a point made by the linguist Whorf thirty years ago. However, selective attention and emphasis are not restricted to language but are characteristic of the rest of culture as well.

The rules governing what one perceives and is blind to in the course of living are not simple; at least five sets of disparate categories of events must be taken into account. These are: the subject or activity, the situation, one's status in a social system, past experience, and culture. The patterns governing juggling these five dimensions are learned early in life and are mostly taken for granted. The "subject" or topic one is engaged in has a great deal to do with what one does and does not attend. People working in the "hard" sciences, chemistry and physics, which deal with the physical world, are able to attend and integrate a considerably higher proportion of significant events observed than scientists working with living systems. The physical scientist has fewer variables to deal with; his abstractions are closer to the real events; and context is of less importance. This characterization is, of course, oversimplified. But it is important to remember that the laws governing the physical world, while relatively simply compared to those governing human behavior, may seem complex to the layman, while the complexity of language appears simple to the physicist, who like everyone else, has been talking all his life. In these terms it is all too easy for the person who is in full command of a particular behavioral system, such as language, to confuse what he can do with a given system, with the unstated rules governing the way the system operates. The conceptual model I am using take into account not only what one takes in and screens out but what one does not know about a given system even though one has mastered that system. The two are not the same. Michael Polanyi stated this principle quite elegantly when he said, "The structure of a machine cannot be defined in terms of the laws which it harnesses."

What man chooses to take in, either consciously or unconsciously, is what gives structure and meaning to his world. Furthermore, what he perceives is "what he intends to do about it". Setting aside the other four dimensions (situation, status, past experience, and culture), theoretically it would be possible to arrange all of man's activities along a continuum ranging from those in which a very high proportion of the events influencing the outcome were consciously considered to those in which a much smaller number were considered. In the United Sates, interpersonal relations are frequently at the low end of the scale. Everyone has had the experience of thinking that he was making a good impression only to learn later that he was not. At times like these, we are paying attention to the wrong things or screening out behavior we should be observing. A common fault of teachers and professors is that they pay more attention to their subject matter than they do to their students, who frequently pay too much attention to the professor and not enough to the subject.

The "situation" also determines what one consciously takes in and leaves out. In an American court of law, the attorneys, the judge, and the jury are impelled by custom and legal practice to pay attention only to what is legally part of the record. Context, by design, carries very little weight. Contrast this with a situation in which an employee is trying to decipher the boss's behavior—whether he is pleased or not, and if he is going to grant a raise. Every little clue is a story in itself, as is the employee's knowledge of behavior in the past.

One's status in a social system also affects what must be attended. People at the top pay attention to different things from those at the middle or the bottom of the system. In order to survive, all organizations, whatever their size, have to develop techniques not only for replacing their leader but for switching the new leader's perceptions from the internal concerns he focused on when he was at the lower and middle levels to a type of global view that enables the head man or woman to chart the course for the institutions. The far-reaching consequences of what is attended can be illustrated by a characteristic fault in Western thinking which dates back to the philosophers of ancient Greece.

Our way of thinking is quite arbitrary and causes us to look at ideas rather than events—a most serious shortcoming. Also, linearity can get in the way of mutual understanding and divert people needlessly along irrelevant tangents. The processes I am describing are particularly common in the social sciences, although the younger scientists in these fields are gradually beginning to accept the fact that when someone is talking about events on one level this does not means that he has failed to take into account the many other events on different levels. It is just that one can talk about only a single aspect of some things (at any moment illustrating the linear characteristic of language).

The results of this syndrome (of having to take multiple levels into account when using a single-level system) are reflected in a remark made by one of our most brilliant and least appreciated thinkers in modern psychiatry, H.S. Sullivan, when he observed that as he composed his articles, lectures, and books the person he was writing to (Whom he projected in his mind's eye) was a cross between an imbecile and a bitterly paranoid critic. What a waste! And so confusing to the reader who wants to find out what the man is really trying to say.

In less complex and fast-moving times, the problem of mutual understanding was not as difficult, because most transactions were conducted with people well known to the speaker or writer, people with similar backgrounds. It lessens the area of discourse (love, business, science)—to get to know each other well enough so that they realize what each person is and is not taking into account. This is crucial. Yet few are willing to make the very real effort—life simply moves too fast—which may explain some of the alienation one sees in the world today.

Programming of the sort I am alluding to takes place in all normal human transactions as well as those of many higher mammals. It constitutes the unmeasurable part of communication. This brings us to the point where it is possible to discuss context in relation to meaning, because what one pays attention to or does not attend is largely a matter of context. Remember, contexting is also an important way of handling the very great complexity of human transactions so that the system does not bog down in information overload.

Like a number of my colleagues, I have observed that meaning and context are inextricably bound up with each other. While a linguistic code can be analyzed on some levels independent of context (which is what the machine translation project tried to accomplish), in real life the code, the context, and the meaning can only be seen as different aspects of a single event. What is unfeasible is to measure on side of the equation and not the others.

Earlier, I said that high-context messages are placed at one end and low-context manages at the other end of a continuum. A high-context (HC) communication or message is one in which moist of the information is either in the physical context or internalized in the person, while very little is in the coded, explicit, transmitted part of the message. A low-context (LC) communication is just the opposite; i.e., the mass of the information is vested in the explicit code. Twins who have grown up together can and would communicate more economically (HC) than two lawyers in a courtroom during a trail (LC), a mathematician programming a computer, two politicians drafting legislation, two administrators writing a regulation, or a child trying to explain to his mother why he got into a fight.

Although no culture exists exclusively at one end of the scale, some are high while others are low. American culture, while not on the bottom, is toward the lower end of the scale. We are still considerably above the German-Swiss, the Germans, and the Scandinavians in the amount of contexting needed in everyday life. While complex, multi-institutional cultures (those that are technologically advanced) might be thought of as inevitably LC, this is not always true. China, the possessor of a great and complex culture, is on the high-context end of the scale.

One notices this particularly in the written language of China, which is thirty-five hundred years old and has changed very little in the past three thousand years. This common written language is a unifying force tying together half a billion Chinese, Koreans, Japanese, and even some of the Vietnamese who speak Chinese. The need for context is experienced when looking up words in a Chinese dictionary. To use a Chinese dictionary, the reader must know the significance of 214 radicals (there are no counterparts for radicals in the Indo-European language). For example, to find the word for star on must know that it appears under the sun radical. To be literate in Chinese, one has to be conversant with Chinese history. In addition, the spoken pronunciation system must be known, because there are four tones and a change of tone means a change of meaning; whereas in English, French, German, Spanish, Italian, etc., the reader need not know how to pronounce the langue in order to read it. Another interesting sidelight on the Chinese orthography is that it is also an art form. To my knowledge, no low-context communication system has ever been an art form. Good art is always high-context; had art, low-context. This is one reason why good art persists and art that releases its message all at once does not.

(Source: Adapted from Hall, E. T.1989. Beyond Culture, New York: Anchor books. pp: 83-92)

After reading activity

1. ***What is the context?***
2. ***What are the characteristics of High-and low-context culture?***
3. ***The following conversation is from the movie*** **Joy Luck Club** (1993). ***The conversation is happening at the dinner table.***

Waverly (the daughter): As is the Chinese cook's custom, my mother always insults her own cooking, but only with the dishes she serves with special pride.

Lindo (the mother): This dish not salty enough. No flavor. It's too bad to eat, but please.

Waverly: That was our cue to eat some and proclaim it the best she'd ever made.

Rich (Waverly's white American boyfriend): You know, all it needs is a little soy sauce.

Waverly: And he proceeded to pour a riverful of the salty black stuff on the platter, right before my mother's horrified eyes.

***Discuss the following question with your classmates*:**

1) Is the dish really bad-tasted? What is Lindo's real intention?
2) Why did Rich respond in that way? What information did he get from Lindo's words?
3) How should Rich response to Lindo's speech in a Chinese way?
4) Use the high- and low-context language theory to analyse the situation.

(3)

Verbal Communication: The Way People Speak

Cultures influence communication styles. Although this point may seem obvious, cultural styles can and do create misunderstandings in conversations among people from different cultures.

For example, consider the following conversation between an Italian and an American. The Italian made a strong political statement with which he knew his American friend would disagree. The Italian wanted to involve the American in a lively discussion. The American, rather than openly disagreeing, said, "Well, everyone is entitled to an opinion. I accept that your opinion is different than mine."

The Italian responded, "That's all you have to say about it?" In general, the American did not enjoy verbal conflicts over politics or anything else. The Italian actually became angry when the American refused to get involved in the discussion. He later explained to the American, "a conversation isn't fun unless it becomes heated!"

What does this example say about culture and its influence on communication? Surely, there are many Americans who do get involved in verbal conflicts over politics, just as there are some Italians who would not become involved. However, the above conversation represents types of communication patterns that are related to cultural differences.

Conversational Involvement

In her book *You Just Don't Understand*, the sociolinguistic researcher Deborah Tannen discusses the notion that people from some cultures value "high involvement" conversation patterns, while others value "high considerateness" patterns. Many people from cultures that prefer "high involvement" styles tend to: (1) talk more; (2) interrupt more; (3) expect to be interrupted; (4) talk more loudly at times; and (5) talk more quickly than those from cultures favoring "high considerateness" styles. Many "high involvement" speakers enjoy arguments and might even think that others are not interested if they are not ready to engage in a heated discussion.

On the other hand, people from cultures that favor "high considerateness" styles tend to: (1) speak one at a time; (2) refrain from interrupting; and (3) give plenty of positive and respectful responses to their conversation partners. Most teachers of English as a Second Language (ESL) in multicultural classrooms have observed that some students become very involved in classroom conversation and discussion, whereas others tend to participate only in a hesitant manner. The challenge for the teacher is not to allow the "high involvement" group to dominate discussions!

The cultures that Tannen characterizes as having "high involvement" conversational styles include Russian, Italian, Greek, Spanish, South American, Arab, and African. In general, the various communication styles in Asian cultures (e.g., Chinese and Japanese) would be characterized as "high considerateness". Mainstream American conversation style would also be characterized as "high considerateness", although it differs significantly from the various Asian patterns. There are important regional and ethnic differences in conversation styles within the United States.

1. Incorrect Judgments of Character

Americans can have problems when talking to each other because of differences. For example, New Yorkers tend to talk faster and respond more quickly ("high involvement") than Californians ("high considerateness"). To some New Yorkers, Californians seem slower, less intelligent, and not as responsive. To some Californians, New Yorkers seem pushy and domineering. The judgments that people make about regional differences within a country are similar to those they make about people from another culture. The reactions to such differences are not usually expressed in the following reasonable fashion: "The way she speaks is different from my way of speaking. She must have had a different cultural upbringing. I won't judge her according to my standards of what is an acceptable communication style."

Instead, people tend to make judgments such as, "she's loud, pushy and domineering," or "he doesn't seem interested in talking. He's very passive and uninvolved." The people interacting are forgetting that their respective cultural styles are responsible, in part, for their mannerisms and habits of communication. The important differences in communication create problems of stereotyping and incorrect judgments among members of diverse groups.

2. Directness and Indirectness

Cultural beliefs differ as to whether directness or indirectness is considered positive. In the mainstream American culture, the ideal form of communication includes being direct rather than indirect. ("Ideal" here means that the culture values this style, although not everyone speaks directly.) There are several expressions in English that emphasize the importance of being direct: "Get to the point! Don't beat around the bush! Let's get down to business!" These sayings all indicate the importance of dealing directly with issues rather than avoiding them. One way to determine whether a culture favors a direct or indirect style in communication is to find out how the people in that culture express disagreement or how they say, "No." In Japan, there are at least fifteen ways of saying "no", without actually saying the word. Similarly, in Japan, it would be considered rude to say directly, "I disagree with you," or "You're wrong."

Many Americans believe that "honesty is the best policy", and their communication style reflects this. Honesty and directness in communication are strongly related. It is no surprising, then, to find out that cultural groups misjudge each other based on different beliefs about directness and honesty in communication.

It is impossible to say that everyone in one culture communicates similarly. Older people often communicate according to more traditional norms than younger people, and, as mentioned, there are regional variations in the way people speak and carry on conversations. In addition, there are gender differences in communication styles.

To generalize (and we do not want to stereotype), American women have traditionally been less direct (i.e., more polite and "softer") than men in making requests, expressing criticism, and offering opinions. However, when talking about emotional issues and feelings, women tend to be more direct than men. In the workplace, women have learned that in order to compete and communicate with men, they have to be more direct when making suggestions, giving criticism, and expressing ideas. In the mid-1980s, "assertiveness training" courses were designed to help women communicate more directly, especially in the business world. In the 1990s, however, there is more recognition of the feminine contribution to work relationships (e.g., nurturing, interpersonal sensitivity, etc.). The emphasis in the workplace is on cultural diversity; women are defined as a "cultural group".

3. Cross-Cultural Implications

Americans may judge members of cultural groups that value indirectness (i.e., hesitating, not "getting to the point", and "beating around the bush") as not being assertive enough. However, many Americans in the business world do not realize that a large percentage of the world's cultures value indirectness and consider it rude to insist on "getting to the point".

When Americans go to work in countries where indirectness is valued (e.g., in Latin America or Asia), they may need to modify their communication style. In such cultures, Americans should not be too direct when giving criticism, making requests, and expressing needs and opinions. Some of the goals of indirect communication include not angering, embarrassing, or shaming another person. North Americans working in Latin America would benefit from understanding the cultural values of "saving face" (and not causing someone else to "lose face"), and maintaining harmony. These two values in personal and business relations almost always mean a more indirect style of communication. (Interestingly, although Latin American conversation style is considered "high involvement", and many Asian styles are considered "high considerateness", they both tend to value indirectness.)

Conversation Structures

Let's look at another example of how people's communication patterns differ: the way people converse. Some foreigners have observed that when Americans hold a conversation, it seems like they are having a ping-pong game. One person has the ball and then hits it to the other side of the table. The other player hits the ball back and the game continues. If one person doesn't return the ball, then the conversation stops. Each part of the conversation follows this pattern: the greeting and the opening, the discussion of a topic, and the closing and farewell. If either person talks too much, the other may become impatient and feel that the other is monopolizing the conversation. Similarly, if one person doesn't say enough or ask enough questions to keep the conversation moving, the conversation stops.

Many North Americans are impatient with culturally different conversation styles simply because the styles are unfamiliar. For example, to many North Americans, it seems that some Latin Americans monopolize conversations, or hold the ball too long. (Remember the "high involvement" style mentioned.) Speaking of her co-workers from several Latin American countries, one North American woman said, "I just can't seem to get a word in edgewise. They seem to take such a long time to express themselves. They give you a lot of unnecessary details." When she talked with them, she became tense, because she found it so hard to participate. Yet she also noted that when they talked to each other, nobody seemed uncomfortable or left out.

The North American woman didn't know how to interrupt the Latin American conversations because North American ways of listening and breaking in are very different. She had been taught to listen politely until the other person had finished talking. (Once again, there are gender differences; it has been observed that men tend to interrupt women more than women interrupt men.) When the North American woman did what was "natural" or "normal" for her (i.e., listen politely without interrupting), she was not comfortable in the conversation with the Latin Americans. The result was that she became more passive in her conversations with her co-workers. The differences between the unspoken rules of conversation of each cultural group interfered with their on-the-job relationship.

1. "Ping-Pong" and "Bowling" Conversation Styles

An example of a conversation style that contrasts with the American "ping-pong" conversation style is formal conversation among the Japanese, which has been compared to bowling. Each participant in a Japanese conversation waits politely for a turn and knows exactly when the time is right to speak. That is, they know their place in line. One's turn depends on status, age, and the relationship to the other persons. When it is time to take a turn, the person bowls carefully. The others watch politely, and do not leave their places in line or take a turn out of order. No one else speaks until the ball has reached the bowling pins. Answers to questions are carefully thought out, rather than blurted out. In a Japanese conversation, long silences are tolerated. Whereas the Americans do not like the feeling of "pulling teeth" in conversations.

The American who is used to the "ping-pong" style of communication is probably going to have some difficulty with someone whose conversational style is like a bowling game. According to some Japanese, Americans ask too many questions and do not give the other persons enough time to formulate a careful answer. The American, however, is not doing something "wrong" or insensitive on purpose. The Japanese feels that the American is pushy and overly inquisitive because of the difference in cultural conditioning.

To the American, the Japanese speaker appears passive and uninterested in the conversation. The Japanese style takes too long for the average American. The Japanese person is not doing anything "wrong" and is no less interested in conversation. Each person has misjudged the other because neither is familiar with their culturally different conversational styles. (Conversely, to many people having "high involvement" styles of communication, the American does not seem pushy and inquisitive. From their viewpoint, the American seems more passive!)

2. Ethnocentric Judgments

The judgments that people make about each other are often ethnocentric. That is, they interpret, judge, and behave in a way that they assume to be normal, correct, and therefore, universal. However, "normal" and "correct" often mean what is "normal" and "correct" in one's own culture. When two people from different cultures communicate, they must continually ask themselves, "do people understand me the way someone from my own culture would understand me?" There may be a gap between what a person is communicating and how people are understanding the message.

People cannot assume that their way of communicating is universal. If people from another culture seem to be communicating in what you feel are "mysterious ways", consider the following four points:

1) It is possible that the way they speak reflects a cultural style.
2) Your success in developing cross-cultural rapport is directly related to your ability to understand others' culturally influenced communication styles.
3) Your ways seem as "mysterious" to others as their ways seem to you.
4) It is often valuable to talk about cultural differences in communication styles before they result in serious misunderstanding.

It is not possible or necessary to know everything about the way a cultural group communicates before having contact with that group. It can take years to understand verbal style differences. However, if you can anticipate differences in communication style, your judgments about people will be more accurate, and you will have fewer cross-cultural misunderstanding.

(Adapted from Levine, D. R. and M. B. Adelman. 1993. *Beyond Language: Cross-cultural Communication*. 2nd ed. Englewood Cliffs, New Jersey: Prentice Hall Regents.)

After reading activity

1. ***Read the list of communication functions below and choose one. In your native language, write a short dialogue containing that function. Then translate the dialogue word for word into English. Find out from your teacher (or any American) if the translation sounds correct. From the direct translations, you should be able to see how culture affects the way we speak.***

Communication Functions

praise	compliment	evaluate
criticize	request	demand
inquire	clarify	correct
give feedback	receive feedback	interrupt
offer	refuse	maintain conversation
disagree	disapprove	agree
express emotion	extend invitations	initiate conversations
end conversations		

2. ***Pick the idioms and expressions from below which reflect the idea of directness in conversation.***

1) Speak up.
2) The mouth is the cause of calamity.
3) Silence is gold.
4) Say what's on your mind.
5) Let's get down to business.
6) Whereas the force of words is soon spent. Far better is it to keep what is in the heart.
7) Those who are glib in their speech and wear an ingratiating expression have little benevolence about them.
8) Don't beat around the bush.
9) It is the duck that squawks that gets shot.

Kaleidoscope

Appropriate and Inappropriate Conversation Topics by Country

Country	Appropriate Topics	Topics to Avoid
Austria	Professions, cars, skiing, music	Money, religion, divorce/separation
France	Music, books, sports, theater	Prices of items, one's work, income, age
Germany	Travel abroad, international politics, hobbies, soccer	World War Ⅱ, personal life
Great Britain	History, architecture, gardening	Politics, money/prices, Falklands War
Japan	History, culture, art	World War Ⅱ
Mexico	Family, social concerns	Politics, debt/inflation problems, border violations
Saudi Arabia	Soccer, travel abroad	Personal family matters, politics
South Africa	Weather, beauty of the country, occupation	Personal questions, political situation, ethnic differences

Verbal Styles by Country

Ethnic Group	Verbal Style
Japanese	• They converse without responding to what the other person says. Emphasis is on nonverbal communication, so they do not listen. • They prefer less talkative persons and value silence. • They make excuse at the beginning of a conversation for what they are about to say. They do not want apologies for what was already said. • They have many different meanings for the word "YES".

Contiued

Ethnic Group	Verbal Style
Mexican	• They seem overly dramatic and emotional to U.S. persons. • They rise above and embellish facts; eloquence is admired. • They like to use diminutives, making the world smaller and more intimate. They add suffixes to words to minimize importance. • They appear to be less than truthful. Their rationale involves two types of reality: objective and interpersonal. Mexicans want to keep people happy for the moment. When asked for directions, if they don't know the answer they will create directions to appear to be helpful.
Chinese	• They understate or convey meanings indirectly. They use vague terms and double negatives; even criticism is indirect. • Harmony is very important. During negotiations, the Chinese state their position in such a way that seems repetitious. They do not change their point of view without discussing it with the group. • They speak humbly and speak negatively of their supposedly meager skills and those of their subordinates and their family.
Arabian	• They encourage eloquence and "flowery" prose. They are verbose, repetitious, and shout when excited. • For dramatic effect, they punctuate remarks by pounding the table and making threatening gestures. • They view swearing, cursing, and the use of obscenities as offensive. • They like to talk about religion and politics but avoid talking about death, illness, and disasters. Emotional issues are avoided. • The first name is used immediately upon meeting but may be preceded by the title "Mr." or "Miss".
German	• In the German language, the verb often comes at the end of the sentence. In oral communication, Germans do not immediately get to the point. • Germans are honest and direct; they stick to the facts. They are low-context people; everything is spelled out. • Germans usually do not use first names unless they are close friends (of which they have few). • They do not engage in small talk; their conversations are serious on a wide variety of topics. Avoid conversations related to their private life.
U.S. American	• Some words are specific to an age group. • Men speak more and more often than women; women are more emotional and use such terms as "sweet", "darling", and "dreadful". • Racial and co-cultural differences in verbal styles exist.

Mini-case Study

After Kukushina, Japan was hit by an unprecedented earthquake, and the American students voluntarily formed a charity committee intending to collect donation for the disaster-struck Japanese people. They invited the only two Japanese students in class to join the committee. Keiko was one of them. Jenny, An American student who is 10 years older than Keiko, was also a committee member. Jenny had once lived in Japan for 3 years. Keiko knew Jenny's life in Japan and also knew she was good at cooking Japanese dishes.

The committee finally decided to hold a Japanese food party to raise the money. At one committee meeting, Jenny brought a food menu to discuss with other members. While the American students were heatedly discussing the issue, Jenny noticed Keiko did not say too much in the whole process. She liked to hear suggestions and advices form Keiko, so, she consciously included her to the discussion by asking for her opinions on things. However, Keiko would mostly respond by saying "it is a good idea!" or "I couldn't agree more!" or "I don't have more to say! I think your idea is great!"

At the same time, Keiko looked a little impatient. In fact, her old friends suddenly dropped by. Because the friend only came to visit thecity for one day and would leave in the next morning, she had to go to meet her. She thought the meeting would be finished in one hour, so she didn't tell the committee about this small incident. But after one hour, the discussion was still on. Finally, Keiko stood up and said: "I am sorry, but I have an appointment and have to go." All of her behaviors and saying made the rest Americans very upset.

Excercises

1.*Discussion.*

1) What do you think of Keiko's behaviors in the meeting? What did she say and do that gave rise to the misunderstanding?

2) What do you think of Jenny's behaviors in the meeting? Why did she act in that way?

2.*Role play.*

Role play the meeting after Keiko left: while American students were complaining about Keiko's rude and uncooperative behaviors, Jenny tried to help to erase the misunderstanding with her knowledge in Japanese conversational style.

After-class Exercises

Reading

How To Use Humor Successfully in Business Communications

by Suzan St. Maur

Yes, trying to raise a laugh does have its place in business and can bring many benefits. But beware, it could land you into hot water, too! Here's how to harness humor to work for you, not against you.

For generations people have been saying that laughter is good medicine.

And now the scientists have taken an interest, it turns out that great-grandma was right. The boffins have discovered that laughter releases helpful goodies in the body which boost your immune system.

In fact, the therapeutic benefits of laughter are now being harnessed by academia and the business community into laughter workshops and other formalized chuckle sessions. Get the workers laughing and you raise productivity, so it seems.

However, it is extremely easy to get humor wrong. And a joke that's sent to someone who doesn't see the funny side will create more ill health through raised blood pressure than a few laughs could ever cure.

So what's the answer? How do we harness humor and make it work for us, not against us?

People often say that the internet's international nature makes it an unsuitable environment for humor for fear of it not translating across national boundaries—and inadvertently causing offense. But there are a couple of simple rules which—although not universal panaceas that always work—can help you use humor without risk.

Use humor about situations, not people. If you think about it, the butt of many jokes and other humor is a person or group of people, so it's hardly surprising that offense is caused. The more extreme types are obvious—mother-in-law jokes, blonde jokes, women jokes, men jokes—but there are many more subtle ones too.

Then there are the nationality gags. I remember in one year hearing exactly the same joke (in three different languages) told by an American about the Polish, by a Canadian about Newfoundlanders, by a French person about Belgians, by a French-speaking Belgian about the Flemish, and by a Flemish person about the Dutch.

Obviously most humor is going to involve people in one way or another. But as long as the butt of the joke is a situation or set of circumstances, not the people, you're far less likely to upset anyone.

And there is an added advantage here. Whoever they are and wherever they come from, people will usually identify with a situation. Take this one for example...

Some people are driving along at night and are stopped by a police car. The officer goes to the driver and warns him that one of the rear lights on his SUV isn't working.

The driver jumps out and looks terribly upset. The officer reassures him that he won't get a ticket, it's just a warning, so there's no problem.

"Oh yes there is a problem," says the man as he rushes towards the back of the car. "If you could see my rear lights it means I've lost my trailer."

As the butt of the joke is the broken rear light and the loss of the trailer, not the policeman or the driver, no-one can be offended. And most people can identify with how that would feel.

The other key issue with humor is wordplays, puns, and anything else that's based on figurative speech, slang, or jargon. The short answer is they don't work internationally. However, if the play or double entendre is in the concept rather than the words, it probably will work.

These may be funny to us, but would not be understood by anyone who is not a good English speaker because there is a play on the words:

Deja moo: The feeling that you've heard this bull before.

The two most common elements in the universe are hydrogen and stupidity.

These, however, probably would be understood because the humor is in the concept, not in the words themselves:

You don't stop laughing because you grow old. You grow old because you stop laughing.

The trouble with doing something right the first time is that nobody appreciates how difficult it was.

Overall, I think it's wise to use humor as a spicy condiment in your business communication. And just as you would with the chili powder, use it in moderation if you don't know the audience well... and if you know they have a very sensitive palate, don't use it at all!

Excercises

1. ***Choose the correct word for each sentence.***

1) laugh, chuckle, giggle

The little girl ____________ while her father tickled her.

Although he tried his best to lower his voice, his ____________ still attracted a lot of attention in the library.

I suggested that he should apologize for his words and he ____________ in my face.

2) humor, joke, gag

That comedian always tells the same ____________.

He played a ____________ on me by pretending he's lost the tickets.

He hasn't got much of a sense of ____________.

2. ***Use the proper form of the word to fill in the blanks.***

1) He gave me a fright by bursting into a sudden ____________ (laugh).

2) They have all the ____________ that a higher income brings, such as new cars, a big house, holidays abroad. (good)

3) The agreement must be ____________ before it can have the force of law. (formal)

4) Her beauty can't make up for her ____________. (stupid)

5) Don't be so ____________ and I was not criticizing you. (sense)

3. ***Translate the following sentences, paying attention to the words in bold type which may have different meanings in different contexts.***

1) He stamped his **butt** on the floor.

2) Poor John was the **butt** of all their jokes.

3) Some people believe human beings can **harness** the nature.

4) The stable boy helps to put a **harness** to the horse.

5) Entrance to the theatre is by **ticket** only.

6) If you leave your car there you might get a parking **ticket**.

4. ***Can you understand the cultural connotation behind the jokes?***

Blonde Jokes:

1) A: how does a blonde try to kill a bird?

B: she throws it off a cliff!

2) A: What do you call it when a blonde dyes her hair brunette?

B: Artificial intelligence.

Ethnic Jokes:

3) Bragging about Japan

There was a Japanese man who went to America for sightseeing. On the last day, he hailed a cab and told the driver to drive to the airport. During the journey, a Honda drove past the taxi. Thereupon, the man leaned out of the window excitedly and yelled, "Honda, very fast! Made in Japan!"

After a while, a Toyota sped past the taxi. Again, the Japanese man leaned out of the window and yelled, "Toyota, very fast! Made in Japan!"

And then a Mitsubishi sped past the taxi. For the third time, the Japanese leaned out of the window and yelled, "Mitsubishi, very fast! Made in Japan!"

The driver was a little angry, but he kept quiet. And this went on for quite a number of cars. Finally, the taxi came to the airport. The fare was US $ 300.

The Japanese exclaimed, "Wah... so expensive!"

Thereupon, the driver yelled back, "Meter, very fast! Made in Japan!"

4) Angering the Irishman

Three Englishmen were in a bar and spotted an Irishman. So, one of the Englishmen walked over to the Irishman, tapped him on the shoulder, and said, "Hey, I hear your St. Patrick was a drunken loser."

"Oh really, hmm, didn't know that."

Puzzled, the Englishman walked back to his buddies. "I told him St. Patrick was a loser, and he didn't care." The second Englishman remarked, "You just don't know how to set him off... watch and learn." So, the second Englishman walked over to the Irishman, tapped him on the shoulder and said, "Hey, I hear your St. Patrick was a lying, cheating, idiotic, low-life scum!"

"Oh really, hmm, didn't know that."

Shocked beyond belief, the Englishman went back to his buddies. "You're right. He's unshakable!"

The third Englishman remarked, "Boys, I'll really tick him off... just watch." So the third Englishman walked over to the Irishman, tapped him on the shoulder and said, "I hear St. Patrick was an Englishman!"

"Yeah, that's what your buddies were trying to tell me."

UNIT 8 Nonverbal Communication: Speaking Without Words

Pre-class Activity

Act It Out

The following are ten situations where you cannot speak a word but only express the meaning by moving your hands. Ask your partner to guess what you want to say.

1. You can't hear your friend's voice.
2. You want a child to come to your side.
3. Your friend has just walked into the class to take an important examination. Wish him or her good luck.
4. Somebody has asked you a question, but you don't know the answer.
5. You signal to your friend that the person on the phone is talking too much.
6. You just realize that you miss a very important date.
7. You signal someone to stop talking.
8. You tell your friend "I love you".
9. Excuse yourself of telling a white lie.
10. You want to take a free ride in a countryside road.

Read to Learn More

Text

Nonverbal Communication: Specific Functions and Patterns

Nonverbal interaction has both cultural-universal and cultural-specific aspects. For example, while all human beings carry the predisposition to express emotions via nonverbal cues, culture shapes the display rules of when, where, with whom, and how these different emotions should be expressed or suppressed. Nonverbal display rules are learned within a culture. Cultural value tendencies (e. g., individualism-collectivism and power distance), in conjunction with many relational and situational factors, influence cross-cultural nonverbal behaviors.

Nonverbal communication is defined as the nonlinguistic behaviors (or attributes) that are consciously or unconsciously encoded and decoded via multiple communication channels. Multiple channels refer to how the meaning of nonverbal messages can be simultaneously signaled and interpreted through various nonverbal mediums such as facial expressions, bodily gestures, spatial relationships, and the environment (physical and psychological) in which people are communicating. Nonverbal communication shares many features with verbal communication; nevertheless, (1) nonverbal messages carry continuous meanings (e.g., via various ranges of tone of voice); (2) they are sent via multiple interaction channels; (3) they have sensory immediacy, appealing to our senses of sight, smell, taste, hearing, and touch; (4) they can be simultaneously decoded (e. g., decoding facial expressions and the tone of voice together); and (5) from a perceiver-centered perspective, nonverbal communication takes place both intentionally and unintentionally. Nonverbal communication is a rich, complex field of study. This section examines the basic functions of cross-cultural nonverbal communication and uses examples from the study of kinesics (facial and bodily movemetns), oculesics (eye contact), vocalice (e.g., tone of voice, volume), proxemics (spatial distance), haptics (touch), environment (e.g. dĕcor, architecture), and chronemics (time) to illustrate the diverse nonverbal function (see belowing Figure).

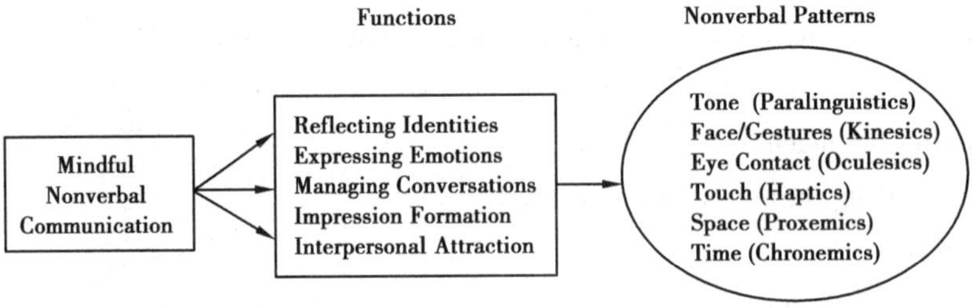

(Figure: Mindful nonverbal communication: Functions and patterns)

Based on previous nonverbal research, the following nonverbal functions are identified: (1) reflecting and managing identities; (2) expressing emotions and attitudes; (3) conversational management; and (4) impression formation and attraction.

Reflecting and Managing Identities

Nonverbal cues serve as the markers of our identities. The way we dress, our accent pattern, our nonverbal way of gesturing tell others something about ourselves and how we want to be perceived. Likewise, we rely on nonverbal cues as "name badges—to discern what groups they [or others] belong to and whether they appear similar or dissimilar to us. This process of identification is at the heart of our self-concept and is a driving force behind our feelings of belonging to valued or stigmatized groups".

Thus, nonverbal cues serve as our identity badges and the identity badges through which we place others into categories (e.g., in-group and out-group). Whenever we come into contact with others, our sex, race, age, face, hair, clothing, body shape, and overall physical attractiveness are visually displayed and then interpreted through the mediation of stereotypes. Our accents, posture, and hand gestures further give our group membership away. According to social perception research, sex and race are the two primary or "primitive" categories that are immediately processed in the first few minutes of an intergroup encounter.

Factors that affect such categorical slotting include the following: (1) contrastive physical cues (such as skin color and facial features); (2) a person's "typicality" as mediated through our stereotypic lenses that she or he "looks like someone from that group"; and (3) nonverbal speech patterns such as contrastive accents, grammar, and manner of speaking. In initial intergroup encounters, the communicators typically perform their nonverbal identity habits (e.g., the use of a habitual tone of voice) without conscious processing. Likewise, we tend to respond to others via our stereotypic group images and expectations rather than responding to personal contact characteristics.

For example, many devout Muslim women wear clothing that is at least ankle length and partially sleeved. They also veil their faces, "wholly or partially, in conservative countries such as Saudi Arabia, Kuwait, the Arabian Gulf states, Yemen and Libya, and tosome degree in Morocco, Algeria, and Tunisia... as an appropriate acknowledgment of the status and nature of women... providing protection for women [from] possible indignities found in outside society. Some women, however, view their situation otherwise and have begun pressing for greater social, legal, and personal freedom".

Thus, adornment features such as clothing, jewelry, cosmetics, and accessories in different cultures also reflect a complex reality—with respect to enhancing, asserting, or reflecting identities. Based on our stereotypic knowledge of a particular group, we look for validation of our expectations via nonverbal cues and surface adornment feature.

Expressing Emotions and Attitudes

It is through nonverbal messages that we infer the feelings and attitudes of the stranger in the interaction. Feelings and attitudes are typically inferred through the nonverbal systems of *kinesics* and vocalics. The term kinesics, derived from the Greek word *kinesis* ("movement"), encompasses all forms of facial, bodily, and gestural movement.

Individualists often think it their right to freely express their personal ideas and feelings, whereas collectivists tend to be more concerned with other people's opinions and reactions. Thus, they guard their emotions more cautiously, especially with in-group members. Furthermore, when perceiving threats in the interaction, individualists tend to be more concerned with expressing and repairing self-focused emotions (e.g., personal anger, frustration, or resentment), whereas collectivist generally are more concerned with other-focused emotions (e.g., relational shame, hurt, or embarrassment).

People from small power distance cultures (e.g., in Australia and Canada) tend to use nonverbal emotional cues to establish equal-status relationships. People from large power distance cultures (e.g., in many Latin and Middle Eastern cultures) tend to use nonverbal emotional cues (e.g., the proper tone of voice) to signify asymmetrical-status relationships. However, misunderstandings or frustrations often occur because cultural members fail to observe and decode the subtle (or not so subtle) nonverbal cues in intercultural episodes. Cultural members tend to use their nonverbal cultural frame of reference to judge the other's "miscued" performance.

In a study probing the emotional experience of generic "feel good" emotions (such as feeling relaxed, elated, and calm), some interesting cross-cultural differences emerge. U. S. college students perceive the generic "feel good" emotions as associated with socially disengaged emotion (such as feelings of pride and superiority). Japanese college students, on the other hand, equate the "feel good" emotions with socially engaged emotions (such as friendly feelings and feelings of respect). It appears that while the decoding of the six facial emotions can be pancultural, the meaning, the circumstances, and the associated tasks that are related to generate such emotions are culture-specific. For individualists, the successful achievement of goals that bring personal recognition and pride make them feel generally good about themselves. For collectivists, the effective achievement of goals that makes the group members feel good about one another generates the general feelings of well-being.

In addition, the meaning of smiles can carry different connotations in different cultures, Within the U.S. culture, a smile can mean joy or happiness. In the Japanese culture, while a smile can be used to signal joy, it can also be used to mask embarrassment, hide displeasure, or suppress anger. In Russia, facial expressions serve as important negotiation cues. U. S. Americans are taught to "open conversations with a smile and to keep smiling. Russians tend to start out with grim faces, but when they do smile, it reflects relaxation and progress in developing a good relationship. Winks and nods are also good signs".

Along with facial expressions of emotions, the human voice carries powerful emotional meaning. In the U. S. culture, soft emotions such as grief and love are expressed through pitch variations. Harsh emotions such as anger and contempt are expressed by changes in volume (i.e., loudness vs. softness). Neutral emotions such as indifference are expressed through tempo changes.

Cultural norms also greatly influence our conversational volume and intensity. While many Southern European cultures (e.g., Greece and Italy) and Arab cultures (e.g., Saudi Arabia and Yemen) tend to value an emotionally engaged, expressive tone of voice when important issues are discussed, many East and Southeast Asian cultures (e.g., Malaysia and Thailand) tend to value a moderating, soft tone of voice for both females and males. According to Nydell, one of the most commonly misunderstood aspects of Arab communication involves the "display of anger". Arabs are not usually angry as they appear to be. Raising the voice, repeating points, even pounding the table for emphasis may sound angry, but in the speaker's mind, they merely indicate sincerity.

In sum, different cultural socialization processes contribute to the display of various facial and vocalic emotional expressions. Consensual meanings of such nonverbal behaviors are perpetuated and reinforced through ongoing cultural activities and interactions. Intercultural nonverbal strains may occur when individualists cannot accurately decode or interpret collectivists, or collectivists cannot fathom the implicit norms and rules that govern individualists' nonverbal expressive mode.

Conversational Management

People generally use kinesics (e.g., hand gestures and body posture) and oculesics (i.e., eye gaze and face gaze) to manage their conversational with others. Hand gestures and body postures have been categorized as emblems, illustrators, regulators, and adaptors.

Emblems are hand gestures that hold specific meanings for members within a culture. They have a direct verbal referent and can substitute for the words that they represent (e.g., the nonverbal peace sign, the hitchhike sign, etc.). They are most often gestures or movements with intentional meanings (e.g., lifted shoulders with palms turned up meaning "I don't know", a common U.S. emblem). They can be recognized by in-group members even when displayed out of context. Emblems typically carry special meanings for members of the in-group. Greeting rituals, beckoning gestures, peace or insult gestures, gang signs, and head movements to indicate "yes" or "no" are all example of emblems.

However, emblems can contribute to intercultural misunderstandings or conflicts. For example, the beckoning "come here" gesture observed in many Asian cultures (e.g., China and Japan) with the palm down and the fingers waving toward the body can signal "go away" to most North Americans. A single hand gesture signifying OK to U.S. Americans in which one raises one's hand and makes a circle between the thumb and forefinger can mean "money" to Japanese, a sexual insult in Brazil and Greece, a vulgar gesture in Russia, or "zero" in French. The Bulgarian turn of the head sideways from left to right, which indicates "yes", means "no" for many other cultures. The "V-for-victory" sign is done by extending the forefinger and index finger upward and apart—the palm may face in or out in the United States; however, in Britain the "V" sign with the palm turned inward (but not outward) connotes an insult. The "thumbs up" gesture used in Canada and the United States to signify approval or encouragement is offensive throughout the Arab world (e.g., in Egypt and Kuwait).

Illustrators are nonverbal hand gestures that are used to complement or illustrate spoken words. They are less arbitrary than emblems. They are the most "pictorial" of all kinesic behaviors, being hand gestures that accentuate a word or phrase. They can also be used to illustrate directions or "draw" a picture of the intended verbal meaning.

Italians have been found to use more broad, full-arm gestures to illustrate their conversations than do U.S. Americans. They also like to "talk with their hands", and most hand gestures are expressive and innocuous. In contrast, Asians tend to use fewer and more restrained hand gestures to complement their conversations than do either U.S. Americans or southern Europeans. They prefer to focus on the interactions and consider that the use of too many hand gestures is distracting, rude, and undisciplined.

Regulators include the use of vocalics, kinesics (especially nonverbal gestures and head movements), and oculesics to regulate the pacing and flow of the conversation. Next to emblems, regulators are considered as culture specific nonverbal behaviors. For example, in international business negotiations, it has been found that Brazilians tend to interrupt twice as much as either Japanese or U.S. Americans during conversations. In addition, Japanese negotiators tend to use silence most, U.S. Americans use it a moderate amount, and Brazilian negotiators almost none at all. Additionally, vocal segregate such as "hai, hai" in Japanese and "uhhuh" in English can be classified as nonverbal regulatory devices. For the Japanese, vocal pause-filler cues such as "hai, hai" mean "I'm hearing you"; however, the literal translation of "hai" means "yes" to Westerners. Within the U.S. culture, ethnic groups such as African American, European American, Latino/a American, and Asian immigrant groups have been found to follow different eye contact norms in regulating conversations. Of the four groups, Latino Americans appear to engage in more intense and prolonged eye contact during conversations than do European American, African American, and Asian immigrant groups, in that order. Furthermore, Asian immigrants and Native Americans have been taught to show respect, especially when conversing with elderly or high-status person, by averting eye contact.

Finally, adaptors are nonverbal habits or gestures that are reactions to internal or external stimuli and are used to satisfy psychological or physical needs. Some are learned within a culture (such as converting the mouth when we cough, or blowing the nose using a handkerchief) and others are more automatic (such as scratching an itch). Most are not intended to communicate a message. However, some of these habits can be considered rude in the context of another culture (e.g., never chew gum in public in France; whistling under any circumstances in India is considered impolite; pointing a finger in the Arab world is considered a rude gesture; and winking may be considered an insult or a sexual proposition in India and Pakistan). Using adaptors in the wrong context or at the wrong time can create great distress and confusion in cultural strangers who are unaccustomed to the display of these nonverbal habits.

Impression Formation and Attraction

When we manage our impressions on the nonverbal level, we are concerned with creating a favorable impression in the presence of others so that they can either be attracted to us or at least find us credible. Impression formation and interpersonal attraction are closely intertwined. Perceived physical attractiveness has been consistently associated with positive impression formation. Cultural values and norms, however, influence the implicit criteria we hold for what constitutes perceived attractiveness or unattractiveness.

In comparing U.S. and Japanese perceptions of attractiveness, U.S. college students have consistently rated smiling faces (both American and Japanese faces) as more attractive, intelligent, and sociable than neutral faces. Although the Japanese students have rated smiling faces as more sociable than neutral faces, they have evaluated neutral faces as more intelligent. Additionally, the Japanese students do not perceive smiling faces as being more attractive than neutral faces.

In terms of the perceived credibility aspect, facial composure and body posture appear to influence our judgments of whether individuals appear to be credible (i.e., having high social influence power) or not credible (i.e., having low social influence power). In some Asian cultures (e.g., South Korea and Japan), influential people tend to maintain restrained facial expressions and postural rigidity. In the U.S. culture, however, related facial expressions and posture are associated with credibility and giving positive impressions.

Overall, we can conclude that perceived attractiveness and credibility are two culturally laden phenomena whose meaning reflects social agreements that are created and sustained through cultural nonverbal practices.

(Adapted and edited from Stella, T.. 1999. *Communication Across Cultures*. New York/London: The Guilford Press, pp. 115-127)

After reading activity

1. ***Questions.***

   1) How do people use nonverbal signals to identify their cultural belongingness?
   2) How different in a way do people from collectivist culture and individualist culture express their emotions?
   3) How many kinds of categories can hand gestures and body postures classified into? What are they? Give an example for each category.
   4) If you are preparing for an interview, how could you make yourself look credible and trustworthy to the interviewers?

2. ***Observation: description and opinion.***

   Scene: A gives a birthday gift to B.

   Act the process out:

   - Greeting
   - Gift-giving
   - Farewell

   The rest of class observes the whole process and discuss the following questions:

   - How close to each other did they stand?
   - How much touching took place?
   - What did you notice about eye behavior?
   - What did B do when he/she got the gift?
   - Could you interpret the social relationships between two people talking (e.g., close friends, students, teacher-student, boyfriend-girlfriend)?

Kaleidoscope

Body Language Around the World

Something as simple as a smile can display friendliness in one culture, embarrassment in another, impatience in a third. Even silence means different things in different places.

Language learners will put a lot of time (and money) into mastering the vocabulary and structure of a foreign language without ever considering these non-linguistic parts of communication.

To help you master these significant parts of communication—or simply avoid making an embarrassing faux pas—here are four non-verbal traits that vary from culture to culture.

Gestures

When trying to communicate through a language barrier, it's natural to use gestures as a way of illustrating your point. We assume it's helpful, since our words are being visually reinforced. Hand motions are, however, culturally relative, and the wrong gesture can inadvertently lead to confusion or offence.

The thumbs-up sign is equivalent to the middle finger in Greece and Sardinia. Tapping your finger to your temple is a gesture to show memory in North America, but suggests insanity in Russia. Even nodding yes or shaking one's head no can be misunderstood abroad. The yes-no gestures are reversed in countries like Bulgaria and Albania. In Turkey, "no" is gestured by nodding the head up and back.

It's not just the individual gestures that can cause miscommunication, but the rate of gesturing. Some societies, like Italy and Spain, are known for talking with their hands. Others are more reserved with body movement as a form of politeness. In parts of East Asia, gesturing is considered boorish behaviour, and would be rude in a professional setting.

Silence

Though it can feel like a void in communication, silence can be very meaningful in different cultural contexts. Western cultures, especially North America and the UK, tend to view silence as problematic. In our interactions at work, school, or with friends, silence is uncomfortable. It is often perceived as a sign of inattentiveness or disinterest.

In other cultures, however, silence is not viewed as a negative circumstance. In China, silence can be used to show agreement and receptiveness. In many aboriginal cultures, a question will be answered only after a period of contemplative silence. In Japan, silence from women can be considered an expression of femininity. Though the North American/European instinct may be to fill the silence, this can be cross-culturally perceived as pushy and arrogant.

Touch

Britain, along with much of Northern Europe and the Far East, is classed as a "non-contact" culture, in which there's very little physical contact in people's daily interactions. Even accidentally brushing someone's arm is grounds for an apology. By comparison, in the high-contact cultures of the Middle East, Latin America, and southern Europe, physical touch is a big part of socialising.

What's more, there are different standards for who touches whom and where. In much of the Arab world, men hold hands and kiss each other in greeting, but would never do the same with a woman. In Thailand and Laos, it is taboo to touch anyone's head, even children.

In South Korea, elders can touch younger people with force when trying to get through a crowd, but younger people can't do the same. Naturally, these different standards of contact can lead to misunderstanding. An Argentinian may see a Scandinavian as cold and aloof, while the Scandinavian may see the Argentinian as pushy and presumptuous.

Eye Contact

In most Western countries, frequent eye contact is a sign of confidence and attentiveness. We tend to assume that a conversation partner who looks away is either disengaged or lying. Of course, this is not the standard around the world.

In many Middle Eastern countries, same-gender eye contact tends to be more sustained and intense than the Western standard. In many Asian, African, and Latin American countries, however, this unbroken eye contact would be considered aggressive and confrontational. These cultures tend to be quite conscious of hierarchy, and avoiding eye contact is a sign of respect for bosses and elders. In these parts of the world, children won't look at an adult who is speaking to them, and nor will employees to their bosses.

Mini-case Study

Chinese actress Fan Bingbing poses on the red carpet before the opening of the 64th Cannes Film Festival in Cannes, France, on May 11, 2011.

The dress Fan Bingbing wore aroused a heat debate. Some praised its beauty, saying it was full of auspicious message; some gave harsh critics, blaming it for misleading the public's understanding of Chinese culture. What did the designer try to communicate with people through this dress? And what is your interpretation of the design?

After-class Exercises

1. ***The following pictures show the greeting customs of some cultures. Would you tell which country or region it comes from?***

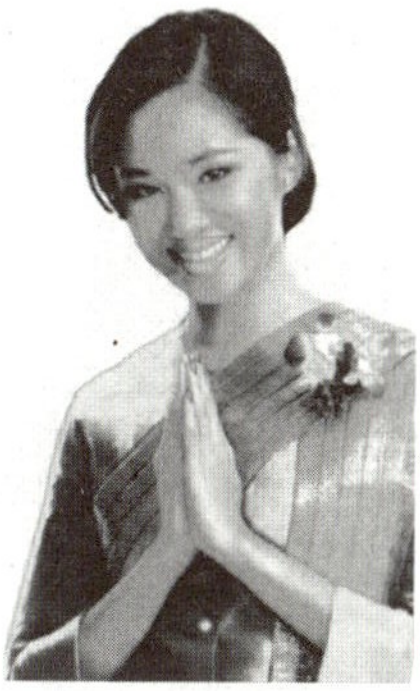

2. ***Tell the cultural differences of the hand gestures below.***

3. ***Explore the different cultural connotation of colours between U.S. American cultures and Chinese Culture.***

UNIT 9 Interpersonal Relationships: Friendship and Facework

Pre-class Activity

Interview Your Classmates by Asking the Following Questions

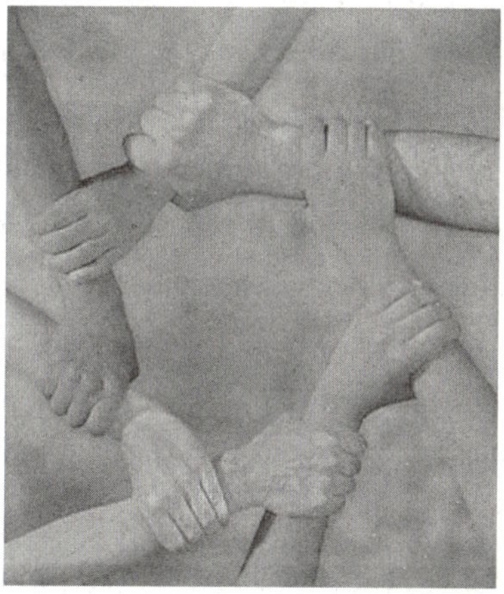

1. How do you define FRIEND?
2. Who can be your friends?
3. How many friends do you have?
4. How long does it take for you to develop friendship with someone?
5. How long can your friendship sustain?
6. What do you do with friends?
7. Do you have foreign friends?
8. Do you like to make friends with foreigners?
9. What main problems do you think you will encounter when making friends with foreigners?

Read to Learn More

Text

Cultural Variations in Interpersonal Relationships

Types of Interpersonal Relationships

Some interpersonal connections occur because of blood or marriage. Others exist because of overlapping or interdependent objectives and goals. Still others bind people together because of common experiences that help to create a perception of "we-ness". However, all interpersonal relationships have as their common characteristic a strong connection among the individuals.

The numbers of interpersonal relationships that you have throughout your life is probably very large. Some of these relationships are complex and involved, whereas others are simple and casual;

some are brief and spontaneous, while others may last a lifetime. Some of these relationships have involved people from different cultures.

Interpersonal relationships between people from different cultures can be difficult to understand and describe because of the contrasts in culturally based expectations about the nature of interpersonal communication. However, regardless of the cultures involved or the circumstances surrounding the relationship's formation, there is always some sort of bond or social connection that links or ties the people to one another. The participants may be strangers, acquaintances, friends, romantic partners, or family or kinship members. Each relationship carries with it certain expectations for appropriate behaviors that are anchored within specific cultures. People in an intercultural relationship, then, may define their experiences very differently and may have dissimilar expectations; for example, a stranger to someone from one culture may be called a friend by someone from another culture.

Strangers

You will undoubtedly talk to many thousands of people in your lifetime and most of them will be strangers to you. But what exactly is a stranger? Certainly, a stranger is someone whom you do not know and who is therefore unfamiliar to you. But is someone always a stranger the first time you meet? How about the second time, or the third? What about the people you talked with several times, although the conversation was restricted to the task of seating you in a restaurant or pricing your groceries, and names were never actually exchanged? Are these people strangers to you? Your answers to these questions, like so many of the ideas described in this book, depend on what you have been taught by your culture.

In the United States, for instance, the social walls that are erected between strangers may not be as thick and impenetrable as they are in some collectivistic cultures. European Americans, who are often fiercely individualistic as a cultural group, may not have developed the strong ingroup bonds that would promote separation from outsiders. Among the Greeks, however, who hold collectivistic values, the word for "non-Greek" translated as "stranger".

Even in the United States, the distinction between stranger and nonstranger is an important one; young children are often taught to be afraid of people they do not know. Compare, however, a U.S. American's reaction toward a stranger with that of a Korean in a similar situation. In Korea, which is a family-dominated collectivist culture, a stranger is anyone to whom you have not been formally introduced. Strangers in Korea are "non-persons" to whom the rules of politeness and social etiquette simply do not apply. Thus, Koreans may jostle you on the street without apologizing, or the Korean anticipates in other ways that he or she may have an ongoing interpersonal relationship with you, elaborate politeness rituals are required.

Acquaintances

An acquaintance is someone you know, but only casually. Therefore, interactions tend to be on a superficial level. The social bonds that link acquaintances are very slight. Acquaintances will typically engage in social politeness rituals, such as greeting one another when first meeting or exchanging small talk on topics generally viewed more impersonal such as the weather, hobbies, fashions, and sports. But acquaintances do not typically confide in one another about personal problems or discuss private concerns. Of course, the topics appropriate for small talk, which do not include personal and private issues, will differ from one culture to another. Among European Americans, it is perfectly appropriate to ask a male acquaintance about his wife; in the United Arab Emirates, it would be a major breach of social etiquette to do so. In New Zealand, it is appropriate to talk about national and international politics; in Pakistan, these and similar topics should be avoided. In Austria, discussions about money and religion are typically sidestepped; elsewhere, acquaintances may well be asked "personal" questions about their income and family background.

Friends

As with many of the other terms that describe interpersonal relationships, friends is a common expression that refers to many different types of relationships. "Good friends", "close friends", and "just friend" are all commonly used expressions among U.S. Americans. Generally speaking, a friend is someone you know well, someone you like, and someone with whom you feel a close personal bond. A friendship usually includes higher levels of intimacy, self-disclosure, involvements, and intensity than does acquaintanceship. In many ways, friends can be thought of as close acquaintances.

Unlike kinships, friendships are voluntary, even though many friendships start because the participants have been thrust together in some way. Because they are voluntary, friendships usually occur between people who see themselves as similar in some important ways and who belong to the same social class.

European American friendships tend to be very compartmentalized because they are based on a shared activity, event, or experience. The European American can study with one friend, play racquetball with another, and go to the movies with a third. This pattern occurs because European Americans typically classify people according to what they do or have achieved rather than who they are. Relations among European Americans are therefore fragmented, and the view themselves and others as a composite of distinct interests.

The Thai are likely to react more to the other person as a whole and will avoid forming friendships with those whose values and behaviors are in some way deemed undesirable. Unlike friendships in the United States, in Thailand a friend is accepted completely or not at all; a person cannot disapprove of some aspect of another's political beliefs or personal life and still consider her or him to be a friend. Similarly, the Chinese typically have fewer friends than European Americans do, but Chinese friends expect one another to be involved in all aspects of their lives and to spend much of their free time together. Friends are expected to anticipate others' needs and to provide unsolicited advice about what to do. These differing expectations can cause serious problems as a Chinese and a European American embark on the development of what each sees as a "friendship".

John Condon has noted that the language people use to describe their interpersonal relationships often reflects the underlying cultural values about their meaning and importance. Thus, Condon says, friendships among European Americans are expressed by terms such as friends, allies, and neighbors, all of which reflect an individualistic cultural value, However, among African Americans and some Southern whites, closeness between friends is expressed by such terms as brother, sister, or cousin, suggesting a collectivist cultural value. Mexican terms for relationships, like the cultural values they represent, are similar to those of African Americans. Thus, when European Americans and Mexicans speak of close friendships, the former will probably use a word such as partner, which suggests a voluntary association, whereas Mexicans may use a word such as brother or sister, which suggests a lasting bond that is beyond the control of any one person.

As interpersonal relationships move from initial acquaintance to close friendship, five types of changes in perceptions and behaviors will probably occur. First, friends interact more frequently; they talk to each other more often, for longer periods of time, and in more varied settings than acquaintances do. Second, the increased frequency of interactions means that friends will have more knowledge about the shared experiences with each other than will acquaintances, and this unique common ground will probably develop into a private communication code to refer to ideas, objects, and experiences that are exclusive to the relationship. Third, the increased knowledge of the other person's motives and typical behaviors means that there is an increased ability to predict a friend's reactions to common situations. The powerful need to reduce uncertainty in the initial stages of relationships suggests that acquaintanceships are unlikely to progress to friendships without the ability to predict the others' intentions and expectations. Fourth, the sense of "we-ness" increases among friends. Friends often feel that their increased investment of time and emotional commitment to the relationship creates a sense of interdependence, so that individual goals and interests are affected by and linked to each person's satisfaction with the relationship. Finally, close friendships are characterized by a heightened sense of caring, commitment, trust, and emotional attachment to the other person, so that the people in a friendship view it as something special and unique.

Intercultural friendships can vary in a variety of ways: whom a person selects as a friend, how long a friendship lasts, the prerogatives and responsibilities of being a friend, the number of friends that a person prefers to have, and even how long a relationship must develop before it becomes a friendship. African American friends, for instance, expect to be able to confront and criticize one another, sometimes in a loud and argumentative manner. Latinos, Asian Americans and African Americans feel that it takes them, on the average, about a year for an acquaintanceship to develop into a close friendship, whereas European Americans feel that it takes only a few months. For intercultural friendships to be successful, therefore, they may require an informal agreement between the friends about each of these aspects for the people involved to have shared expectations about appropriate behaviors.

Dynamics of Interpersonal Relationships

Interpersonal relationships are dynamic. That is, they are continually changing, as they are pushed and pulled by the ongoing tugs of past experiences, present circumstances, and future expectations.

Leslie Baxter suggests that the changing dynamics in interpersonal relationships are due to people's attempts to maintain a sense of "balance" among opposing and seemingly contradictory needs. These basic contradictions in relationships, called "dialectics", create ongoing tensions that affect the way people connect to one another. Three dialectics have been identified as important in interpersonal relationships: autonomy-connection, novelty-predictability, and openness-closedness. Each of the dialectics has corresponding cultural-level components.

The *autonomy-connection dialectic* is perhaps the most central source of tensions in interpersonal relationships. Individuals inevitably vary, at different moments of their interpersonal relationships, in the extent to which they want a sense of separation from others (autonomy) and a feeling of attachment to others (connection). Note the words in the previous sentence; both types of interpersonal needs, though they may seem contradictory, occur simultaneously. As we implied in our discussions of individualism-collectivism, a culture teaches its members both the "correct" range of autonomy and connection and how these should be expressed when communicating with others. Thus, while the general level of autonomy desired by someone from an individualistic culture may be relatively high, one's specific needs for autonomy and connection will vary across time and relationships.

The *novelty-predictability* dialectic relates to people's desire for change and stability in their interpersonal relationships. All relationships require moments of novelty and excitement, or they will be emotionally dead. They also require a sense of predictability, or they will be chaotic. The novelty-predictability dialectic refers to the dynamic tensions between these opposing needs. The cultural dimension of uncertainty avoidance provides a way of understanding the general range of novelty and predictability that people desire. At specific moments within each relationship, however, individuals can vary in their preferences for novelty and predictability.

The *openness-closedness* dialectic relates to people's desire to share or withhold personal information. To some extent, openness and self-disclosure are necessary to establish and maintain relational closeness and intimacy. However, privacy is an equally important need; the desire to establish and maintain boundaries is basic to the human condition. For instance, a person may be open to interpersonal contact at certain moments, or with specific individuals, or about certain topics. There will also be times when that person may want to shut the office door or find another way to lessen the degree of interpersonal contact. The openness-closedness dialectic operates not only within a relationship but also in decisions about the public presentation of the relationship to others. Individuals in interpersonal relationships must continually negotiate what kinds of information about their relationships they want to reveal or withhold from others. Several cultural dimensions may affect openness-closedness. Collectivist cultures, for instance, with their tightly knit ingroups and relatively large social distances from outgroups, typically encourage openness within the ingroup and closedness to outgroup members. Alternatively, cultures that value large power distances may expect openness within interpersonal relationships to be asymmetric, such that those relatively lower in social status are expected to share personal information with their superiors.

Each of these relational dialectics, and others as well, contributes to a dynamically changing set of circumstances that affect what people expect, want, and communicate in interpersonal relationships. As the following section explains, how people in interpersonal relationships maintain an appropriate balance among these dialectics relates to their maintenance of face.

The Maintenance of Face in Interpersonal Relationships

A very important concept for understanding interpersonal communication among people from different cultures is that of face, or the public expression of the inner self. Erving Goffman defined face as the favorable social impression that a person wants others to have of him or her. Face therefore involves a claim for respect and dignity from others.

The definition of *face* suggests that it has three important characteristics. First, face is *social*. This means that face is not what an individual thinks of himself or herself but rather how that person wants others to regard his or her worth. Face, then, always occurs in a relational setting. Because it is social, one can only gain or lose face through actions that are known to others. The most heroic deeds, or the most bestial ones, do not affect a person's face if they are done in complete anonymity. Nor can face be claimed independent of the social perceptions of others. For instance, the statement "no matter what my teachers think of me, I know I am a good student" is not a statement about face. Because face has a social component, a claim for face would occur only when the students conveys to others the idea that teachers should acknowledge her or his status as a good student. In this sense, the concept of face is only meaningful when considered in relation to others in the social network. Consequently, it differs from such psychological concepts as self-esteem or pride, which can be claimed for oneself independently of others and can be increased or decreased either individually or socially.

Second, face is an *impression*, which may or may not be shared by all, that may differ from a person's self-image. People's claims for face, therefore, are not requests to know what others actually think about them; instead, they are solicitations from others of favorable expressions about them. To maintain face, people want others to act toward them with respect, regardless of their "real" thoughts or impressions. Thus, face maintenance involves an expectation that people will act as though the others are appreciated and admired.

Third, face refers only to the *favorable* social attributes that people want others to acknowledge. Unfavorable attributes, of course, are not what others are expected to admire. However, cultures may differ in the behaviors that are highly valued, and they may have very different expectations, or norms, for what are considered to be desirable face behaviors.

Facework and Interpersonal Communication

The term facework refers to the actions people take to deal with their own and other's face needs. Everyday actions that impose on another, such as requests, warnings, compliments, criticisms, apologies, and even praise, may jeopardize the face of one or more participants in a communicative act. Ordinarily, say Brown and Levinson,

> *People cooperate (and assume each other's cooperation) in maintaining face in*

interaction, such cooperation being based on the mutual vulnerability of face. That is, normally everyone's face depends on everyone else's being maintained, and since people can be expected to defend their faces if threatened, and in defending their own to threaten other's faces, it is in general in every participant's best interest to maintain each other's face.

The degree to which a given set of actions may pose a potential threat to one or more aspects of people's face depends on three characteristics of the relationship. First, the potential for face threats is associated with the control dimension of interpersonal communication. Relationships in which there are large power or status differences among the participants have a great potential for people's actions to be interpreted as face-threatening. Within a large organization, for instance, a verbal disagreement between a manager and her employees will have a greater potential to be perceived as face-threatening than will an identical disagreement among employees who are equal in seniority and status.

Second, face-threat potential is associated with the affiliation dimension of interpersonal communication. That is, relationships in which participants have a large social distance, and therefore less social familiarity, have a great potential for actions to be perceived as face-threatening. Thus, very close family members may say things to one another that they would not tolerate from more distant acquaintances. Relationships where strangers have no formal connection to one another but are, for example, simply waiting in line at the train station, the taxi stand, or the bank, may sometimes be seen as an exception to this general principle. As Ron Scollon and Suzie Wong-Scollon suggest, "Westerners often are struck with the contrast they see between the highly polite and deferential Asians they meet in their business, educational and governmental contacts, and the rude, pushy, and aggressive Asians they meet on the subways of Asia's major cities." At many train stations in the People's Republic of China, for example,

People are not in the midst of members of their own community, so the drive to preserve face and act with proper behavior is much lower. Passengers usually wait in waiting rooms until the attendant moves a barrier and they can cross the area between them and the train. The competition is quite fierce as passengers rush toward the train with their luggage, and they have little regard for the safety of other passengers. Often, fellow travelers are injured by luggage, knocked to the ground, or even pushed between the platform and the train, where they fall to the tracks.

Third, face-threat potential is related to culture-specific evaluations that people make. That is, cultures may make unique assessments about the degree to which particular actions are inherently threatening to a person's face. Thus, certain actions within one culture may be regarded as face-threatening, whereas those same actions in another culture may be regarded as perfectly acceptable. In certain cultures, for instance, passing someone a bowl of soup with only one hand, or with one particular hand, may be regarded as an insult and therefore, a threat to face; in other cultures, however, those same actions are perfectly acceptable.

Stella Ting-Toomey and Min-Sun Kim both suggest that cultural differences between individualism and collectivism affect the facewrok behaviors that people are likely to develop. In individualist cultures, concerns about message clarity and preserving one's own face are more important than maintaining the face of others, because tasks are more important than relationships, and individual autonomy must be preserved. Consequently, direct, dominating, and controlling face-negotiation strategies are common, and there is a low degree of sensitivity to the face-threatening capabilities of particular messages. Conversely, in collectivist cultures, the mutual preservation of face is extremely important, because it is vital that people be approved and admired by others. Therefore, indirect, obliging, and smoothing face-negotiation strategies are common; direct confrontations between people are avoided; concern for the feelings of others is height-ended; and ordinary communication messages are seen as having a great face-threatening potential.

Facework and Intercultural Communication

Competent facework, which lessens the potential for specific actions to be regarded as face-threatening, encompasses a wide variety of communication behaviors. These behaviors may include apologies, excessive politeness, the narration of justifications or excuses, displays of deference and submission, the use of intermediaries or other avoidance strategies, claims of common ground or the intention to act cooperatively, or the use of implication or indirect speech. The specific facework strategies a person uses, however, are shaped and modified by his or her culture. For instance, the Japanese and U. S. Americans have very different reactions when they realize that they have committed a face-threatening act and would like to restore the other's face. The Japanese prefer to adapt their messages to the social status of their interaction partners and provide an appropriate apology. They want to repair the damage, if possible, but without providing reasons that explain or justify their original error. Conversely, U.S. Americans would prefer to adapt their messages to the nature of the provocation and provide verbal justifications for their initial actions. They may use humor or aggression to divert attention from their actions but do not apologize for their original error.

As another example of culture-specific differences in facework behaviors, consider the comments that are commonly appended to the report cards of high school students in the United States and in China. In the United States, evaluations of high school students include specific statements about students' strengths and weaknesses. In China, however, the high school report cards that are issued at the end of each semester never criticize the students directly; rather, teachers use indirect language and say "I wish that you would make more progress in such areas as..." in order to save face while conveying his or her evaluations.

Facework is a central and enduring feature of all interpersonal relationships. Facework is concerned with the communication activities that help to create, maintain, and sustain the connections between people.

(Adapted from Lustig, M. W. & J. Koester, 2010. *Intercultural Competence: Interpersonal Communication Across Cultures*. 6th Ed. Boston: Pearson, pp. 245-262.)

After reading activity

In the following situations, an American businessman who visits China the first time sees things which confuse him a lot. Xiao Zhang, his Chinese interpreter, is supposed to explain those situations from a culture perspective. Work out a conversation and role play the following situations:

Scene 1:

While Mr. Smith was walking on the street, he was surprised to see women walking hand in hand. Sometimes, he even saw men walking side by side with one man's arm wrapping around the other man's shoulder. Mr. Smith thought they were gays and lesbians, but Xiao Zhang said they were simply friends.

Mr. Smith: ______________________

Xiao Zhang: ______________________

Scene 2:

Mr. Smith was invited to dine with the heads of some Chinese companies in a restaurant. The Chinese hosts came over to make toasts time and time again. Although he had explained that he was not good at drinking, they insisted that he should at least finish one cup with each of them. He consulted his Chinese colleague whether he should drink or not. The latter advised him to do so in order to establish a friendly long-term *guanxi* with their companies and also give faces to those leaders.

Mr. Smith: ______________________

Xiao Zhang: ______________________

Scene 3:

At the end of the dinner, he saw two men at the next table arguing about something loudly, with the bill in one man's hand, but minutes before, they were talking to each other happily. Again, he was confused and turned to his Chinese colleague for answer. But again, Xiao Zhang told him fighting to pay the bill was very common between friends in China.

Mr. Smith: ______________________

Xiao Zhang: ______________________

Scene 4:

Mr. Smith caught a cold. He had to stay in hotel and put off some important meetings. One leader from the Chinese company dropped by without a previous notice. He asked him not to worry about the meeting and said he could arrange someone to take him to the hospital if he wanted. When

Mr. Smith refused that, he asked him to stay in bed, drink more water and take a lot of rest. Mr. Smith was a bit uncomfortable. Back in America, only someone's mother would speak like that. He told this to Xiao Zhang, and Xiao Zhang said caring for the subordinates and friends like that was also very common in China.

Mr. Smith: ____________________

Xiao Zhang: ____________________

Kaleidoscope

(1)

The American Concept of Friendship

International visitors sometimes feel betrayed by Americans who they meet and who seem so kind and interested at first but who later fail to allow new acquaintances to really get to know them as individuals. That initial friendly "Hi!" may come to seem dishonest or misleading as the small talk continues and Americans' ideas about important topics remain hidden. "They seem cold, not really human," one Brazilian woman said. "Americans just can't let themselves go."

The Nature of Friendship

Many Americans seem unavailable for the close friendship that many foreigners have had (and taken for granted) at home and assume they will find in the United States. Sometimes people simply lack the time required to get to know another person well. Many have moved from one place to another in the past, assume they will do so again, and thus may prefer not to establish intimate friendships that will be painful to leave. Americans have also been taught, as was discussed, to become independent, self-reliant individuals. Although such individuals may have a large circle of friends, they are likely to avoid becoming too dependent on other people or allowing others to become dependent on them. With the exception of their immediate families, they often remain apart from others, because they most likely have not learned to do otherwise.

This is not to say that Americans never have close friendships. They do. Such relationships are relatively rare, however, and can take years to develop. Moreover, the close friendships Americans form often differ from those to which many foreigners are accustomed. Because Americans are so busy with school, their careers, and other activities, it is not uncommon for them to go weeks, months, or even longer without seeing their close friends, especially if they live in different cities. They might or might not be in regular contact with their friends by telephone, e-mail, Twitter, Facebook, blog, or even, in ever fewer instances, a letter written on paper and sent through the mail. The most important characteristics of a close friendship, for many Americans, are the freedom to discuss private, personal matters as well as the persistence of the relationship over time and distance.

It is important to remember that there are exceptions to these generalizations. Some Americans are indeed willing to devote the time that is necessary to get to know new acquaintances well and to develop close friendships with them. They will talk openly about personal thoughts and feelings that other Americans rarely reveal.

Compartmentalized Friendships

Americans typically assume that when people gather to socialize, they will undertake some activity together. They may go to a restaurant for lunch or dinner, go to a movie, play cards, engage in or watch sports, or "have a few drinks". Americans do not usually assume that it can be pleasant or rewarding to sit and talk with other people for extended periods. (Americans would probably say "just sit" and "just talk".) Their discomfort with such a lack of structured activity is often evident if they are forced to sit and interact with people they do not know fairly well.

In some ways teenagers are an exception to what has just been said. They often "hang out" (or just "hang") with other teens—at a mall, in someone's car, or at one of their homes. Even so, the sense they often convey is not that they are enjoying each other's idle company but that they are looking for something to do or waiting for something to happen.

When they are apart from their peers, many teenagers—and not only teenagers, as things are evolving—use electronic social networks or other electronic means to "keep in touch" with their "friends" or "followers" and possibly arrange to get together in person.

Perhaps because of their emphasis on "doing things" with friends, Americans typically develop what have been called compartmentalized friendships. That is, they tend to have different friends with whom they engage in different activities. For example, Americans might have friends with whom they study, others with whom they go to the gym, and still others with whom, they go shopping or dancing on Saturday nights. Likewise, coworkers who eat lunch together every day and occasionally go out for drinks after work may never set foot in one another's homes or meet members of one another's families.

Gender Roles and Friendship

In many countries, a friend must be a person of one's own gender. Most Americans, though, believe it is possible to have friends of the opposite sex, and they do not generally assume that a male and female will participate in sexual activity if they are alone together. This is not to say that Americans see no sexual component in a male-female friendship; they believe the people involved are capable of showing the restrain and maturity necessary to avoid sexual interaction if it is inappropriate for the situation. Thus, male and female business colleagues might travel to a conference together without any one's assuming that their relationship entails sexual contact.

(2)

Courtesy, Schedules, Gifts

Courtesy

Among Americans, being courteous has a number of elements:

- Acknowledging another person's presence or arrival, either verbally (if not with "hi!" then with "hello", "good morning", or some such greeting) or nonverbally, with a direct look, a nod, or a brief smile (By contrast, someone's departure from a group or gathering does not necessarily require explicit acknowledgement—as does a German's departure from a group of Germans, for example—except that a guest leaving a social event is expected to say thank-you and goodbye to the host.)
- Participating in at least a bit of small talk with people when one expects to be in their presence for more than a few minutes
- Using vocabulary, tone of voice, and vocal volume no less respectful than those used with peers; never "talking down" to others, issuing commands in an officious way, or in any way treating others as though they were inferior
- Saying "please" when making requests and "thank you" when requests are granted by anyone, including service people such as servers, taxi drivers, and hotel desk clerks and maids
- Saying "you're welcome" in response to a "thank you"
- Taking a place at the end of a line (what people in much of the world call a queue) and waiting patiently when a group of people have lined up for service or attention

Schedules

Considerate people will be mindful of other people's domestic schedules and will not telephone too early, too late, or during mealtimes. Most Americans take breakfast between 7:00 and 9:00 A.M., lunch at noon or shortly thereafter, and an evening meal (called dinner in some parts of the country and supper in others) between 6:00 and 7:00 P.M. on Sundays, all meals may be taken somewhat later.

It is generally a good idea to make telephone calls to a person's home between the hours of 9:00 A.M. and 9:00 P.M. (except at mealtimes), unless there is reason to believe that everyone in the family will be awake before or after those hours.

Gifts

Comparatively speaking, Americans give gifts on a relatively small number of occasions and to a relatively small circle of people. Since offering gifts to people who do not expect them can be mutually embarrassing and can even lead to the suspicion that the gift-giver is seeking to influence the recipient inappropriately, international visitors will want to be mindful of Americans' practices concerning gifts.

Generally, Americans give gifts to relatives and close friends. Frequently they give gifts to hosts or hostesses (flowers, wine, or candy are common). They do not normally give gifts to teachers (except perhaps elementary-school teachers, who sometimes receive gifts from children in their classes), business colleagues, or other people who might be in a position to grant or withhold favorable treatment (such as a good grade in a class or a sales contract). In fact, giving gifts to people who are in a position to grant or withhold favors can be construed as an improper attempt to gain favor. Many states have laws strictly limiting the value of gifts that public employees can accept.

Christmas comes close to being a national gift-giving day in the United States. Except for adherents of non-Christian religions, Americans exchange Christmas gifts with relatives, close friends, and sometimes schoolmates and business associates. Other typical gift-giving occasions include birthdays, graduations, weddings, and childbirths. Some people give gifts on Mother's Day, Father's Day, and Valentine's Day. A "housewarming" gift is sometimes given to people who have moved into a new home.

Americans try to select a gift they believe the recipient could use or would enjoy. People are not expected to give expensive gifts unless they can readily afford them. "It's the thought that counts," Americans say, not the amount of money the gift cost. Increasing numbers of Americans give gift cards or gift certificates, which allow their recipient to choose whatever merchandise or service they prefer.

Internet gift registries take the guesswork out of deciding what gift to buy for the registrant. Such registries are most often used in relation to weddings, where the bride and groom indicate which of a store's item of merchandise they would like to have. Gift-givers then log on to the store's website and select from the items so identified. In some cases the store will send the gift, with a card, to its intended recipient.

Many Americans send Christmas cards to their friends, acquaintances, distant family members, and in some instances, business colleagues. Those who follow a non-Christian religion may send a holiday card to convey "season's greetings" or some such nonsectarian message. Along with cards, many people send a "Christmas letter" or "holiday letter" that summarizes their family's activities of the past year—normally emphasizing the positive and minimizing the negative. The advent of e-mail and economic hardship has caused many Americans to shorten their list of recipients for Christmas cards. They may send e-mails (which, of course, are free) instead, or simply fall out of touch.

(Adapted from Althen, Gary & Janet Bennett. 2011. *American Ways: A Cultural Guide to the United States*. 3rd Ed. Boston/London: Intercultural Press.)

Mini-case Study

Dinner at A Friend's

Janice Linzwe was a young engineer working for a pump manufacturing joint venture operation in Wuhan. She had studied Chinese for two years at college and felt her competency with Chinese was growing rapidly; she was even learning a little of the local dialect. She felt lucky that her husband, George Carter, had been willing and able to make the move with her and that he, too, seemed to be enjoying his English-teaching job and their new life in Wuhan.

Janice felt that she got along well professionally with her Chinese colleagues, but she wished she could get friendlier with them; they seemed a little distant and cautious. She was really pleased, therefore, when Liu Lingling, another engineer, who seemed slightly less shy than the rest, invited Janice and George to her home for dinner one Friday night after work.

Lingling met them at the bus stop and took them to her home, a sparsely furnished but very clean two-room apartment. She briefly introduced them to her husband, Yang Feng, who was busy in the tiny kitchen, and then invited Janice and Gorge to sit down in a room where there was a table with eight plates of various cold dishes on it. She served them some tea and then disappeared for fifteen minutes. Just when Janice was about to get up and ask if anything was wrong, Liu Lingling returned and added hot water to their tea. In answer to their offers, Liu Lingling assured them that she and her husband didn't need any help in the kitchen. She pointed out a new CD player that she and Yang Feng had recently purchased and their 35-inch color TV set and invited the American couple to have a look at them. Then she disappeared again. After nearly three quarters of an hour, Lingling reappeared. The three of them sat down and began to eat. Yang Feng came into the room from time to time to put a hot dish on the table. Most of the food was wonderful, but there was far too much of it. Janice passed on the eel and the sea cucumber, and George skipped from one dish to another. Both George and Janice were full before half the dishes had been served. Also, they couldn't help wishing that Yang Feng would sit down, so that they could get a chance to talk to him. When he finally did come in from the kitchen, he ate a bit and then turned on the TV, fiddling with knobs to show them all of the features. Lingling proceeded to demonstrate the CD player, and then it was late and time to go home.

Although they felt vaguely depressed by their first social encounter with Liu Lingling and Yang Feng, they felt that they should return the dinner invitation, so they invited the Chinese couple over two weeks later. George and Janice decided to introduce their new friends to an American meal. George scoured the hotels and grocery stores that catered to Western tastes. He was excited to find some black olives, tomato juice, soda crackers, and even some tolerable cheese. Janice made spaghetti and a salad. She even concocted some dressing from oil, vinegar, and some sweet-smelling but unidentified herbs she found on the market. George and Janice were pleased with their efforts. When Liu Lingling and Yang Feng arrived, they were obviously impressed by the apartment. They asked the prices of the carpet, CD/tape player, TV set, and the vacuum cleaner. They pressed every button on every appliance, and Janice was glad the food processor was tucked away in a kitchen cupboard. They nibbled without enthusiasm at the appetizers, but Janice was pleased that they seemed to be having fun. She did, however, refused politely their questions about the cost of everything.

The Chinese couple seemed a little confused when both Janice and George sat down to the meal, and Liu Lingling asked who was doing the cooking. She still looked confused, even after Janice and George had explained who had prepared the food and dishes. The two Chinese ate just a tiny bit of spaghetti and didn't finish the salad on their plates. George urged them to eat more, but they continued to refuse and to look expectantly. George and Janice explained the origin of each of the foods served, found out where Liu Lingling and Yang Feng's families were from, and learned quite a bit about Yang Feng's job as a physics professor. They also answered questions about their own families and hometowns. When it seemed everyone was done, George cleaned the table and Janice served coffee and some chocolate pastries she had found in a hotel bakery. Liu Lingling put four spoonfuls of sugar in her coffee and drank about a third of it. Yang Feng took one sip and left the rest. Neither ate more than two bites of pastry.

After they left, George said to Janice, "at least we had a chance to talk." But Janice replied in a dismayed voice, "we left their place so full that we couldn't walk, but they're going to have to eat again when they get home. What went wrong?"

As a friend of George and Janice's, how would you explain to them what cultural assumptions were at work that kept them from having a successful dinner party with their new friends?

(Adapted from Linell, Davis. 2001. *Doing Culture: Cross-Cultural Communication in Action*. Beijing: Foreign Language Teaching and Research Press.)

After-class Exercises

Reading

How to Make Friends with People from a Different Culture?

There are some rules as follows for you if you want to make friends with people from a different culture:

Appreciate the Person

Most Americans like to be recognized as individuals as someone special with unique personalities. Therefore, never say "you're from America so I want to be your friend." Also don't imply that the reason why you approached them is that you wanted someone to practice your English with. That turns people off. Instead try saying, "you seem like a real nice and interesting person and I would like to get to know you better." This way, they are much more inclined to be friendly because you see them as a three dimensional person and appreciate them for who they are in the inside. And by doing so, you not only learn about Americans and practice your English, but also gain a real friend in the process.

Quit Calling Them Foreigners

Please avoid calling a foreigner a foreigner especially in his face. The word makes people feel like an outsider, and even unwelcome, suggesting separation and insurmountable differences, as well as widening an already existing gap in the situation. When Americans travel, they rarely say, "I'm foreign to your place." They tend to say, "I'm new in town. I'm new here." The reason is that new and unfamiliar things can become old and familiar. But can foreign things become native? Aha? You catch my drift.

Just Do It

Some students like to be told about American culture but are less interested in spending the time and the effort to actually experience it. As Americans always say, "get your hands dirty." You should have first hand and hands-on experience, or you'll never really know anything.

Find that Common Language

Now I must stress the importance of finding a common language. By that I don't mean English, Chinese, German, French, etc. I mean finding something you have in common with another person on a spiritual and philosophical level: likes, dislikes, worldviews, ways of thinking, and attitudes toward life. And to start, you must first enhance your knowledge of the particular culture from which your potential new friend comes from.

Multiple Choices

1. The underlined sentence "get your hands dirty" means to ________.
   A. get involved
   B. start with dirty work
   C. talk about American culture
   D. not to wash your hands too often
2. Americans prefer to make friends with those who________.
   A. avoid talking about their homeland
   B. recognize their personalities
   C. obey rules of communicating with friends
   D. needn't practice English while playing together
3. According to the passage, which of the following is seen as friendly?
   A. I am longing to make friends with an American.
   B. This is my friend Tom, who is a foreigner.
   C. There must be a gap between us in many things.
   D. You've got a great personality.
4. In the last paragraph, the author suggests we should ________.
   A. learn at least one foreign language well
   B. find common interests or opinions with our potential new friend
   C. make sure we can understand each other
   D. ask where our potential new friends come from

Movie Theatre

Saving Face is a 2004 film directed by Chinese American Alice Wu. The story is about how a Chinese mother and her daughter struggle to keep their secrets and save faces for their family.

Watch this movie and discuss how face works in Chinese culture.

UNIT 10 Work: Practices and Attitudes

Pre-class Activity

The "Competent" Employee

Some American and Japanese college students were in the countryside spending long hot days replanting mountainsides after a forest fire. Each group was assigned daily chores back at the lodge.

Group 3 was responsible for cleaning the camp van every evening, vaccuming and polishing till it shone inside and out. It was tedious work, especially after a rough day laboring on the mountain.

One day all the students stayed at the camp and didn't go out to work with the villagers. At 6:00 P.M., the Japanese senior male students brought out beer and cards and told the women to go cook and the groups to go do their chores.

The Americans in Group 3 grinned and said, "Lucky us, no chores! We didn't use the van today." Then the head senior male student got up and in a fury shouted at them not to be irresponsible, and to go do their job.

Angrily, the Americans went outside and found the Japanese woman student in their group silently cleaning the van all by herself.

Upon reading the story, please put yourselves into the shoes of each cultural group of students, namely, the American students, the Japanese male student and the Japanese female student. Write down what they would possible think of in such a situation. One has been given as a reference. Finally, from those thoughts of Japanese students, try to work out what characters of employees are more expected in the Japanese culture.

The Americans probably thought / felt:	The Japanese senior male students may have thought / felt:	The Japanese woman student may have thought / felt:
■ Why are the men students sitting around making the women and American students work? Not FAIR. ■ ____________ ■ ____________	■ Everyone has their jobs, their roles. Women cook and clean. Men are responsible for the whole program. ■ ____________ ■ ____________	■ Didn't want to interfere with men's roles as leaders. ■ ____________ ■ ____________

Read to Learn More

Text

Work: Practices and Attitudes

Cross-Cultural Implications of the Job Search

"Knock rather on opportunity's door if you wish to enter." "Job hunting" in the United States or in an American organization outside of the United States is a challenging experience for Americans, but it is especially so for people from other countries. A personal contact, such as a friend or relative, can be of help in informing someone of a job opening and possibly helping the job applicant obtain an interview. However, this kind of "connection" (i.e., friend or family member) does not usually affect hiring decisions. Sometimes, immigrants in the United States put too much hope into what they think are good job connections, and they do not fully realize how much they will have to rely on themselves to find a job. One of the biggest shocks some immigrants have upon arriving in the United States is the discovery that the government, schools, and even job placement centers do not hand people jobs on "silver platters".

Steps to Find a Job

The search for a skilled or professional job in the United States may first require foreign visitors or new immigrants to receive some additional training if their skills are not marketable in the United States. After that, the job search consists of a minimum of four steps: (1) preparation; (2) networking; (3) resumé development; and (4) the interview.

1. **Preparation**: This involves identifying one's skills and the range of work one is capable of doing. It includes locating all possible sources for learning about job availability (e.g., the classified ads in newspapers, job placement agencies, and "headhunters"). It is also beneficial to learn something about the companies, agencies, or organizations to which one is applying for work. (Information about major corporations and organizations is available in most libraries.)

2. **Networking**: People usually find jobs on the basis of their performance at an interview, their education, and their work experience. However, first it is important to let others know that one is looking for a job; this increases the likelihood that an employer and a potential employee will be brought to one another's attention. To "network" is to meet people who have similar professional interests and to widen one's circle of acquaintances for the purpose of learning about job opportunities. The more people one knows (and informs of one's job search), the more successful that search is likely to be. Participating in professional organizations and even doing volunteer work can help a job seeker make his or her capabilities known. Having the contacts, however, is only the first step, and does not guarantee getting a job.

3. **Resumé Development**: In some countries, a resumé is not used as an instrument for finding a job. In the United States, however, it is one of the most important ways to "sell oneself" to a prospective employer. A resumé is a one-or two-page summary of professional goals or objectives, education, previous jobs, professional skills, accomplishments, and honors. Resumés occasionally include a little information about personal interests and hobbies.

The resumé is used to communicate quickly and easily with a prospective employer. It should be visually attractive and factually correct. In a resumé, people should present their experience and accomplishments very positively. However, "padding one's resumé" (exaggerating one's experience and accomplishments) is not ethical. A person who greatly exaggerates or lies on a resumé can later be fired, especially if the worker lacks the skills claimed. The same holds true for the cover letter that should accompany the resumé. This letter should describe accurately and briefly a person's professional background, and also mention the position or job in which the applicant is interested. These are special techniques for writing resumés and cover letters; foreign-born job applicants would be well advised to consult books on the subject and to seek help from professional resumé-writing services or career centers.

4. **The Interview**: The best interview is one in which there is two-way communication between the employer and the job applicant. Often there is some "small talk" at the beginning of the interview (e.g., "Did you have trouble finding the company?"). This "small talk" is actually very important, because the applicant's answers may indicate how easily the person can converse. A job seeker who appears unfriendly or unsociable may not be offered a position, even if the person is the most qualified. Employers look for people who seem to be likeable and easy to work with as well as technically competent.

The first few minutes of the interview are very important when it comes to making a good impression. (Some say that the first thirty seconds are crucial.) A smile and handshake are expected after the job applicant walks into the prospective employer's office. In addition, the applicant must pay attention to certain areas related to personal appearance and hygiene. The following list is not intended to insult readers who consider the information obvious:

1. Neatly trimmed hair and beard
2. Clean fingernails
3. Polished shoes
4. Clean and ironed dress or suit and tie
5. Fresh breath
6. An absence of body odors (Americans use a great deal of deodorant!)
7. An absence of strong-smelling perfume, cologne, or after-shave
8. Only a modest amount of jewelry

During the interview, a supervisor or manager (and sometimes other employees) will ask the applicant questions that must be answered fully (but without excessive detail). It is important to watch the employer's face for nonverbal cues as to whether enough has been said. It may be helpful to say something like, "Have I given you enough information, or would you like me to elaborate?" Some questions an applicant may be asked, in either a one-on-one interview or a group interview, include:

1. Tell me (or us) about yourself.
2. What do you know about this company (organization, etc.)?
3. What are your strengths and weaknesses? What do you do best?
4. In which areas do you need more experience?
5. Why did you leave your last job?
6. What are your interests outside of work?
7. How does your education and work experience relate to this job?
8. What are your career plans?
9. What do you expect to be doing in five years?

Some people may have difficulty answering certain questions because of their cultural perspectives. In cultures where humility and modesty are virtues (e.g., in several Asian cultures), the question "What are your strengths?" could be embarrassing. In many cultures (not only Asian), people are taught not to talk or boast about their individual accomplishments. Imagine how difficult it would be for someone raised with the cultural values of humility and modesty to respond to a person of a higher status with something like, "I'm really good at administration." Or, "In my last job, I was the most productive employee in my department." Yet, during an interview, an employer often wants the job candidate to talk about his or her accomplishments. In an American interview, applicants must learn to present themselves in the most positive light. This is a challenge for many people from other countries.

As was mentioned, part of the preparation for an interview involves learning about the organization. The job applicant should have questions prepared for the potential employer. If the applicant has no questions about the organization, the employer may think that the person is not really interested in the job. Asking an employer about the company's product, the size of the various departments, or the method of production, for example, demonstrates the job hunter's interest.

Employer-Employee Relationships

One of the first things that foreign-born individuals notice in American companies and organizations is the casual nature of the employer-employee relationship. Among employees of different status, foreigners often observe a great deal of informal interaction (including chatting and joking). It is not always clear to outsiders who is in charge.

Subordinates often call their superiors by their first names. Many foreign-born professionals find it difficult to become accustomed to his practice, and some add "Miss" or "Mr." to the first name. However, this usage (e.g., "Miss Sue" or "Mr. Michael") is very unfamiliar to Americans. Similarly, most American supervisors do not like to be called "Sir" or "Ma'am." It is common, for example, for Filipino employees (i.e., new immigrants) to use these as terms of respect. However, for most American managers, "Sir" and "Ma'am" convey a position of subservience, which goes against the American cultural value of egalitarianism.

Some supervisors and managers have an open-door office policy whereby employees may enter without appointments. This is unusual for those coming from cultures in which the society emphasizes rank and hierarchy. Again, the American value of egalitarianism manifests itself in casual and informal behavior among people of different status. However, even in the United States, a subordinate is not equal to the boss. The latter has more power, earns a higher salary, and can make decisions about hiring and firing. There is a formal chain of command; status and hierarchy in Untied States organizations do exist. However, outward appearances (i.e., people interactions) do not make this fact obvious.

On-the-Job Communication Skills

What do American employers say about their foreign-born employees with regard to communication at work? One of the first "complaints" one hears is, "Why do some foreign employees say, 'Yes, I understand,' when in fact they do not understand? If I explain something to an American and it is unclear, he or she will say, 'wait, I didn't understand that. Could you go over it again?" Most American managers and co-workers do not understand some of the unspoken rules of communication that accompany superior-subordinate relationships in other cultures. For example, for many Chinese and Vietnamese people, saying to a supervisor, "I do not understand," is considered rude. This may indirectly imply that the supervisor did not explain clearly, which could be insulting, however, Americans expect immediate feedback, especially when it concerns understanding an explanation, process, or procedure at work.

Similarly, people may want to know others' opinions or reactions. In meetings, co-workers (or bosses) may ask each other, "What do you think of...?" or, "What is your reaction to...?" People from some other cultures, such as the Japanese, may tend to hesitate or give an answer that Americans consider to be indirect or noncommittal. They may use more silence than Americans are used to, and say something like, "It is difficult to say," which means, "I do not wish to respond now." Some Japanese people may feel that it is inappropriate to offer an opinion if a person of a higher status is present. Additionally, the Japanese person may want to give a carefully considered answer. In contrast, many Americans like to discuss their preliminary reactions and opinions even before having all the facts.

In American business meetings, people are expected to participate verbally, or else others may think that they are uninterested in the meeting. Active participation involves the following:

1. Initiating discussion, bringing up new ideas and topics, and making suggestions
2. Asking people for opinions, information, and explanations
3. Offering opinions and information when needed
4. Repeating ideas, information, and explanations for the rest of the group when something has not been understood
5. Summarizing information to make sure that a point has been understood
6. Encouraging people to speak by being cooperative and by accepting different points of view

If an employee appears to be passive in meetings (i.e., not participating verbally), Americans may feel that the person is not contributing to the meeting.

Time Considerations in Workplace

Promptness and punctuality are major expectations in the American workplace. People who keep appointments are considered to be dependable, and those who do not are seen as unreliable. It is considered polite to call if one is going to be even a few minutes late. Arriving ten minutes late to a scheduled business appointment (without having called ahead of time) is considered rude and converys a lack of organization. Some companies have been known to fine their executives for tardiness toward meetings. This American cultural concern with every minute contrasts with other cultures' views about time. In many parts of Latin America, for example, arriving thirty to forty-five minutes late is not necessarily seen as disrespectful. Saying that one ran into an old friend could be a sufficient excuse for tardiness but such an explanation would not be acceptable in the American work-a-day world, where "time is money".

The American workday usually begins at 8:00 A.M., 8:30 A.M., or 9:00 A.M., not at 8:10, 8:40, or 9:10. An employer who notices that an employee is regularly coming in several minutes late may give the employee a warning to be on time. In many countries, employees feel that they can stop working if the boss is not around. Of course, this also happens in the United States but Americans (especially professionals) feel they are not using their time well if they are not productive during most of the day. Perhaps because the American culture values daily progress, there is a great emphasis on not wasting time.

In the workplace this value translates into a need for saving time, budgeting time, accounting for time, and allotting time for various activities. In business, time is carefully scheduled. Many people use appointment calendars that are printed with fifteen-, thirty-, and sixty-minute time slots. At meetings, people often decide ahead of time how many minutes they will spend on each item on the agenda. Many workers have eight-to-five jobs with two fifteen-minute coffee breaks (one mid-morning and one mid-afternoon), and a forty-five minute or one-hour lunch break. These employees must "punch the clock" every time they enter and leave their workplace. Work and play or work and social life are seen as distinct activities.

Some of the time-consuming pleasantries that one sees in the business world in other countries are not part of the American business culture. For example, in an effort to "get down to business", Americans do not spend a lot of time getting to know each other well before they do business. This is in contrast to Middle Eastern, Latin American, and Asian cultures where social and personal relations often must precede business relations. People from outside the United States find the pace of life in the American business world (and in people's social and personal worlds as well) to be hectic and stressful. America time has been characterized as a river flowing quickly away from people. In contrast, in other parts of the world (e.g., India), time is seen more as a pool of water that does not go anywhere. The pace of life in the American work world require adjustment for those with a more relaxed view of time.

The "Work Ethic" and Materialism

Originally, attitudes toward work in the United States were greatly influenced by the "work ethic", which motivated people to work hard to become successful. This ethic, which originated with the Puritan colonists from England, was a sign of God's favor. Work was thus imbued with the quality of goodness. Those who achieved success were among God's "chosen" and would go to heaven.

It would be naïve, if not incorrect, to say that today the work ethics is the main motivation for work. There is, rather, an "achievement motivation" that drives people to work hard in the United States. A strong value is placed on productiveness; people who are admired in the work world are those who can produce something tangible. This achievement orientation (or the tendency to "do" and "make") results in part from American materialism, which is an outcome of the work ethics. The harder one works, the more successful one will be. Success brings material rewards, which can be proof of hard work. (This is, however, only a partial, simplistic explanation of American materialism; some materialism is based on a need for status. In addition, much of the tendency toward materialism is a result of advertising and the desire to acquire objects to enhance the quality of life.)

(Adapted from Levine, D.R. and M. B. Adelman. 1993. *Beyond Language: Cross-cultural Communication*. 2nd ed. Englewood Cliffs, New Jersey: Prentice Hall Regents.)

After reading activity

1. Quotations on Work

The followings are religious, literary, and comical quotations on the subject of work. Read them and discuss the questions that follow.

You shall gain your bread by the sweat of your brow.

(*Genesis* 3:19)

Hire yourself out to work which is beneath you rather than become dependent on others.

(*Talmud*)

You work that you may keep peace with the earth and the soul of the earth.

(Kahlil Gibran)

Work and love—these are the basics. Without them there is neurosis.

(Theodor Reik, *Of Love and Lust*)

Nothing is really work unless you would rather be doing something else.

(Sire James Barrie)

You can't eat for eight hours a day nor drink for eight hours a day nor make love for eight hours a day—all you can do for eight hours is work. Which is the reason why man makes himself and everybody else so miserable and unhappy.

(William Faulkner)

2. Discussion

1) What does each of these quotations say about the nature of work?

2) Do they reflect your feelings about work?

3) Do you know any quotes or expressions about work in your language?

3. Job Interview

Suppose you are going to a job interview, how do you answer the following questions?

1) What is your greatest strength?

2) What is your greatest weakness?

3) Why are you leaving or have left your job?

4) Why do you want this job?

5) Why should we hire you?

6) How do you handle stress and pressure?

7) Describe a difficult work situation / project and how you overcame it.

8) How do you evaluate success?

9) What are your goals for the future?

Kaleidoscope

Interviewing Advices

- **Australia**

Pre-Interview Preparation

As part of your interview preparations, you should research the company's philosophy, market strategy and plans for future growth. Visit the organization's website and read any marketing material directed at the company's clients—you may find the latest annual report especially useful.

Interview Conduct

Although business in Australia often is conducted in an open and informal environment, you should maintain a completely professional demeanor and show the utmost courtesy and respect. Project a reserved attitude; Australians dislike arrogant or impolite behavior.

The Interview

You should be prepared to answer a variety of questions. Employers often try to assess an applicant's ability to respond quickly, asking hypothetical questions that require improvisation. Interviewers in Australia typically will ask process-related questions, such as "Tell me about a situation where you have had to be proactive", or "Explain how you resolved a situation with a difficult client".

Post Interview

It is a good practice immediately after the interview to review the questions that were asked and write down what you can remember. This will be helpful if you are called back for a second interview, because it allows you to go over the questions and answers from the initial interview, evaluate your performance and improve on deficiencies—not only for a possible second interview, but when preparing for future interviews as well.

- **Brazil**

Pre-Interview Preparation

When researching a company, you should focus especially on aspects that relate to your occupation. For example, if your position is related to finance, read financial reports (annual reports), generally available on the company's website; if it's engineering, seek information about the company's logistics and industrial operations.

Interview Conduct

Personal appearance is very important in Brazil; it is essential that you dress appropriately and nicely for an interview. Try to get information about the usual dress code for the company—this is important because it reflects the corporate culture.

The Interview

Interviews can be lengthy—up to two hours in some cases, so it is important to keep a reasonably free schedule on an interview day. There is a good chance the proceedings will run beyond the scheduled time, as additional tests may be applied before or after the interview, including language, psychological or logic tests.

Post Interview

After the interview, you may send a message of appreciation by email, thanking the interviewer for the opportunity to be considered for the job.

Selection-process feedback is not a common practice in Brazil.

- **France**

Pre-Interview Preparation

Establishing and nurturing social relationships is very important in France, and networking can be crucial in the job-seeking process. While more than 30 percent of jobs are filled through speculative applications (i.e., applications sent not in response to published job advertisements but aimed at any potential current or future openings within the organization), a comparable number are filled through personal contacts.

Interview Conduct

Business attire is conservative in France; it is appropriate to dress formally for an interview. The French are well dressed and well groomed.

The Interview

In a multinational or a larger organization, the interview procedure usually starts with some psychological or technical tests. The next step is a face-to-face interview. Two to four interviews are usually held for a position, with attention being paid primarily to your personality.

Post Interview

It is not appropriate to call others outside the department to follow up on questions and issues not discussed during the interview. This "going behind the interviewers' backs" could be considered offensive.

- **India**

Pre-Interview Preparation

Rehearse in advance of the interview. Anticipate possible questions and answer them aloud, or write the answers down. This can help improve confidence.

Interview Conduct

It is very important to arrive on time for your interview, so allow extra travel time in case of unavoidable delays. Before the interview, double-check the interviewer's contact number, address and directions, and the contact number of the person who set up the interview, if different from the interviewer.

The Interview

The interview process in India usually includes one or more interviews and, increasingly, psychometric testing. This consists of verbal, numerical and language testing, as well as personality profiling. Interviewers generally will focus on education and the skills and experience the position demands.

Post-Interview

Do not wait more than a day or two to send a thank you email or letter. It should not include any type of inquiry regarding when the interviewer might call or what chance you have of being hired.

- **Japan**

Before the interview, you should research and learn as much as possible about the prospective employer. Studying the company website, reviewing company press releases and speaking to current or former company employees are considered good preparation. If the target company operates stores, hotels or restaurants, take the time to visit at least one or two of them. Learning as much as possible about the company's protocols will help in preparing for the interview.

Pre-Interview Preparation

Punctuality is a must in Japan. Being late is regarded as rude. One should plan his or her travel time to arrive at the meeting location about 15 minutes ahead of schedule. In case one's transportation is delayed or other unforeseeable circumstances don't allow for an on-time arrival, calling the company to alert the interviewer(s) is acceptable. It is wise to get a location map with the closest subway station exit in advance of the meeting and use it as a reference. Most companies provide detailed access information on their homepages. Locations can be difficult to find in complicated urban areas. After arriving at the building early, the applicant should not ask to see the person responsible for the interview until just a few minutes prior to the scheduled time. As unprofessional as a late arrival time can be, arriving too early and expecting immediate attention can also create a negative first impression.

Interview Conduct

The first meeting, which may last 30 to 60 minutes, allows the interviewer to form an initial impression of you as a potential employee, to confirm your skills and motivation, and to review your résumé. If you are from a foreign country, you likely will be asked why you are looking for a job in Japan.

Demonstrating good communication skills and business etiquette during the interview often is as important as impressive credentials. A Japanese interviewer will pay close attention to manners, posture and how well you keep up with the pace of the interview. It's important to remember that your character will be judged thoroughly but with subtlety.

The Interview

The first interview is usually conducted by one person, or possibly by two people. A second and third interview might follow. Some companies have a lengthy interview process of up to six sessions that could involve many people. Hiring an employee is considered to be a group decision, so it is important for you to emphasize and demonstrate an ability to be a team player.

Interviews are typically conducted in meeting rooms. You should stand up when an interviewer enters the room, and be conscious of maintaining good posture and a calm and polite demeanor. When you sit, keep your knees together and rest your hands on your lap or on the table, without appearing unnatural.

- **The United States**

Pre-Interview Preparation

Companies usually interview jobseekers in person and by telephone. Many companies conduct phone interviews, allowing them to quickly and inexpensively interview a large number of applicants and select the most desirable candidates. Excellent performance in a phone interview can help a jobseeker earn an invitation to a subsequent in-person interview. In-person interviews are typically used to make hiring decisions, and a jobseeker's performance in such an interview usually determines whether he/she is chosen for the position. Video interviews are a relatively recent innovation that allow an employer to interview a candidate over the Internet by a video conferencing call. Employers may use these interviews to narrow a large list of job applicants and select final-round candidates; some employers may use video interviews to make a final hiring decision.

Interview Conduct

Punctuality is absolutely essential in the United States, especially for a job interview. It is a good idea for a candidate to arrive ten minutes before the interview and check in with the receptionist, but to not arrive earlier. However, a candidate must be prepared to wait for the interviewer, who often has a very full schedule of interviews.

The Interview

During an interview, a job candidate should display confidence, optimism and a team-oriented mindset, as most American employers seek positive, upbeat and energetic employees. Making direct eye contact with interviewers while speaking and listening is vital, as it demonstrates respect, attention and truthfulness. Employers may interpret a jobseeker's failure to make eye contact as a sign of disinterest, a lack of confidence or dishonesty.

It is appropriate for jobseekers to claim credit for their professional accomplishments and achievements in the interview. Truthfully communicating ambitions and successes is also acceptable in a job interview, as American employers perceive such statements as demonstrating the jobseeker's self-confidence.

Post-Interview

After an interview, it is polite and appropriate to send a short, personal note to the interviewer thanking them for their time and consideration, and reiterating interest in the position. If interviewed by a panel, each interviewer should receive a unique thank-you note. These thank-you notes may be electronic or handwritten, should include details about the topics of conversation in the interview and should be sent within a day or two of the interview. Many job candidates neglect to send thank-you notes. Sending a thank-you note demonstrates diligence and follow-through skills that can distinguish a candidate from other job applicants.

Mini-case Study

Spanish Fury over Chinese Shoes

Several hundred people have taken to the streets for a second day in the Spanish town of Elche to protest against Chinese-owned shoe firms.

Elche is the capital of Spain's footwear industry and has been hard hit by Asian competition.

Some protesters held banners reading "Chinese out"—others smashed windows.

Last week, the protest took a more menacing turn when two Chinese-owned warehouses and a lorry belonging to a Chinese entrepreneur were set on fire.

The attacks caused damage estimated at hundreds of thousands of euros.

Several arrests were made, but the Chinese government has asked the Spanish authorities to compensate the businesses for their losses and to safeguard Chinese citizens and their property in Spain.

Elche, located in the south-east of the country, is the capital of Spain's once flourishing footwear industry.

Many Spanish manufacturers blame their current crisis on cheap Asian imports.

Questions for discussion

1. Look for more information about the shoe-burning event from other media.
2. What is the way of doing business that Chinese people conduct for thousands of years? Why did the Spanish people dislike it?
3. Some demonstrator said: "They should work the same as us." What does this mean? How do Spanish work?
4. Was this conflict simply a matter of business? Could you review it from a cultural perspective?
5. What can Chinese merchants learn from this vicious event?

After-class Exercises

Reding

(1)

Five Things You Owe Your Employer—And Five You Don't

Back in the old days there were working hours. You went to work and then around five p.m., you packed up your stuff and went home. If there were an emergency you might stay until five-thirty.

Those days are gone! White-collar work, sometimes called Knowledge Work, is never done. Your immediate To-Do list might have twenty items on it, but right behind the immediate To-Do list is a supplemental To-Do list with another forty action items on it and after that list is done, there's a third one waiting.

The old rules have changed completely. My teenagers work at retail stores and restaurants. Their workday ends when they clock out but more importantly, they don't take their work home with them. The rest of us do.

We lie in bed and wonder what to do about a billing issue or a complicated client problem. We might spend the whole weekend catching up on our business email correspondence, but we still have to be at our desk on time on Monday morning!

What does your paycheck get your employer—what are your obligations toward your job? Sometimes it's hard to tell. Some managers are beyond demanding. They want you to pass up important family obligations, even ones you've scheduled weeks in advance, to take care of something they missed on their own To-Do list.

Other leaders are more chilled. They realize that you have a life outside of work. Sometimes your life at work and your happiness at home rely on the luck of the draw in the form of the manager you get. That's unacceptable! We are adults.

A new muscle all of us are growing is the muscle called Setting Boundaries.

You can't set boundaries at work until you have a clear sense of what's reasonable and what's unreasonable when it comes to your commitment to your job. To help clarify the often murky—but essential! —demarcation between your work and your life, here's our list of Five Things You Owe Your Employer and Five Things You Don't.

Five Things You Owe Your Employer

Your Best Work Every Day

If you hate your job, start a stealth job search on the side, but don't slack off on your current role. That isn't fair to your employer, its customers or your teammates. It's not fair to yourself. As long as you have the job, put your heart into it!

My motto is this: An employee's job is to give his or her best work every day. A manager's job is to give the employee a good reason to come back to work tomorrow.

Your Creative Solutions

Work is a place to solve problems, bigger and thornier problems all the time. You learn something new and grow your flame a little bit more every time you solve a problem at work.

Even though a job description might be boring, it's still in your best interest to bring your whole brain and heart to your role, as long as you have it.

The Truth

You owe your employer the truth about things that happen at work—whether anyone is dying to hear the truth, or not. When you speak up, your muscles grow.

If it feels scary to speak up, as it often does, think about this: the only way you can solve a problem is by addressing it. If you're sick of pushing a rock uphill and sharing your ideas with people who don't want to hear them, that's a sign from the universe. Don't waste your emotional energy on people who don't want to look at problems and surmount them. Start looking for a new job, instead!

TLC

If it were your company, you'd want your customers, teammates and equipment to be well cared for. When you take a job, it's your role and your desk—take good care of everything that comes across the desk and everyone you work with!

Your Integrity

When you're burned out on a job, it's a stress-reliever to tell your friends how tough you've got it. Eventually, if they're good friends, they're going to say "dude, you have to stop talking about it and DO something."

Complaining about your employer isn't a solution to your problem, and worse than that, it tarnishes your brand as a person with integrity. Hate the job, or a client project? Don't slime them—move on and find something that suits you better.

Five Things You DON'T Owe Your Employer

Your Contacts

In lots of sales jobs and recruiting jobs, your contact list is part of what your employer expects to receive when you get hired. When you take a new job, clarify everybody's expectations with respect to your precious contact list. Unless it's been clearly communicated, your contacts are your own.

If your employer has an employee referral bonus program and you want to participate, go ahead and spread the news about job openings at your workplace, and with luck get paid for it. Otherwise, it's not ethical for your employer to expect you to peddle its products to your friends, or give up your networking contacts to pad its prospect list.

Your Health

The tragedy of the white-collar working world is that we pretend our bodies don't exist. Your brain can't function unless your body gets rest and exercise. It's not right for your employer to expect you to trash your health for the job. Speak up if you're not feeling well.

Don't let a weenie manager browbeat you into coming to work sick and infecting your co-workers, or worsening your own health. If they won't let you work from home when you're under the weather or take a sick day, get your resumé up to date.

Your Personal Life

Everyone needs to learn the script we call "it's Impossible" to deal with managers who ask you what you've got scheduled at night or on the weekend that would keep you from working extra hours.

What you have planned in your personal life is nobody's business but yours. Here's the script:

BOSS: Joe, can you stay late tonight to get those invoices out?

YOU: Not tonight, but I can do them tomorrow.

BOSS: What's going on tonight?

YOU: Unmovable plans, but don't worry—I'll do it tomorrow.

Don't start explaining that your kid has a hockey match or your wife's barbershop chorus has a dress rehearsal that you have to attend because you can't make the concert. The minute you open that vault, you can kiss your personal priorities goodbye.

Learn to say "wish I could! —but it's impossible" with a smile on your face.

Unearned Loyalty

Be wary of any employer that tells employees they should be loyal, just because they work there. Loyalty, like respect, is earned. You might be loyal to a boss who's always had your back, but that's different than being loyal to a corporation or an institution.

If you get a call from a headhunter about a job that sounds interesting, it's your right to call back and learn everything you can. You don't have to stay with a sinking ship and be the person who turns the lights out.

That's what "stay bonuses" are for.

It's appropriate and ethically correct to take care of your own and your family's interests before your employer's, and that's what anyone would do unless there is personal loyalty in place—loyalty that's been earned by past actions.

Run away from people who tell you where they think your loyalties should lie.

Your Soul

Your job might include unpleasant aspects, like bureaucratic processes or boring meetings, but your job shouldn't require you to pretend to be someone you're not. If you wake up at night with your heart beating too fast because you can't stand the person your job requires you to be, get out!

You have one lifetime. You get to make your mark here on our planet, and that means you get to make choices, and you must. You don't have time or energy to waste with people who don't get you and value you the way you are right now.

The story is about setting boundaries around your personal life, so that you can spend more time with your family. Also, we are all like the baby in the image, learning new things and growing new muscles in the new-millennium workplace.

Multiple choices

1. What do the sentences "Some managers are beyond demanding... Other leaders are more chilled." mean?

   A. Some managers like to give orders, but others do not speak to you at all.

   B. Some managers may inspect every work you did, but some ignore you.

   C. Some managers give their employees too much work without considering their private life; some managers may respect employees' personal time at home and give reasonable workload.

   D. Some managers treat their employees too warmly; some managers treat the employees too cold.

2. What does the sentence "A new muscle all of us are growing is the muscle called Setting Boundaries" mean?
   A. A kind of new muscle called Setting Boundaries would grow in our body if we eat properly.
   B. All of us have a potential to set boundaries for our body muscles.
   C. The growing of our muscles has a boundary.
   D. We should cultivate our courage of setting a line between work and family life.
3. In the sentence "If you're sick of pushing a rock uphill and sharing your ideas with people who don't want to hear them, that's a sign from the universe." What does the underlined part mean?
   A. The writer indicates that expressing one's opinions is very painful.
   B. The writer indicates that persuading people to listen to you is very tiring.
   C. The writer indicates that some job is very difficult.
   D. The writer indicates a situation in which you try in vain to arouse people's attention to solving a problem.
4. What does the abbreviation "TLC" possibly stand for in the context?
   A. Total Lung Capacity.
   B. Tender Loving Care.
   C. Thin-layer Chromatography.
   D. Talcum.
5. Which of the following statement is true?
   A. If you have decided to quit a job, it is not a necessary to do everyday work seriously.
   B. Whenever you solve a problem at work, your capability will grow stronger a bit.
   C. You should be nice to your colleagues in case you need their help in the future.
   D. Complaining about your employer will make yourself heartbroken.
6. What should you do with your contact list when you transfer to a new workplace?
   A. You should keep the contact list a secret.
   B. You need to go publishing it.
   C. You shouldn't unveil your contacts until your position in the new company is secure.
   D. You shouldn't unveil your contacts until your boss communicates with you.
7. If you are sick, the writer suggest you ________.
   A. bring your work back and do it at home
   B. go to work and infect the other workers
   C. tell your boss the weather today is not good for working
   D. write it down in your resumé
8. How do you say NO to the extra workload given by your boss?
   A. Tell him the reason directly.
   B. Say NO directly.
   C. Politely refuse him by telling him you have already had an arrangement and promise him you will finish the work tomorrow.
   D. Tell him if he asks you to do extra work you will quit the job.

9. Which of the sayings about loyalty are not true?
   A. If an employee leaves his old job, he will become a man lack of loyalty.
   B. Pay your loyalty to someone in the company is more acceptable than pay your loyalty to the company.
   C. Loyalty is gained through previous actions.
   D. If you think a new job will bring more benefits to your family, it is all right to get it, because you should be also loyal to your family's wellbeing, which is more important than that of your company.
10. What can be a signal telling you to quit the current job?
   A. There is bureaucracy in your workplace.
   B. There are too many boring meetings in your workplace.
   C. You have nightmares often at night.
   D. You feel you are losing the true self and you are not happy with that.

(2)

Lifetime Employment in Japanese Companies

In most large Japanese companies, there is a policy of lifetime employment. What this means is that when people leave school or university to join an enterprise, they can expect to remain with that organization until they retire. In effect, the employee gets job security for life, and can only be fired for serious mistakes in work. Even in times of business recession, he or she is free from the fear of being laid off.

One result of this practice is that the Japanese worker identifies closely with his company and feels strong loyalty to it. By working hard for the company, he believes he is safeguarding his own future. It is not surprising that devotion to one's company is considered a great virtue in Japan. A man is often prepared to put his firm's interests before those of his immediate family.

The job security guaranteed by this system influences the way employees approach their work. They tend to think in terms of what they can achieve throughout their career. This is because they are not judged on how they are performing during a short period of time. They can afford to take a longer perspective than their Western counterparts.

This marriage between the employee and the company—the consequence of lifetime employment—may explain why Japanese workers seem positively to love the products their company is producing and why they are willing to stay on after work, for little overtime pay, to participate in earnest discussions about the quality control of their products.

Multiple choices

1. Lifetime employment in the Japanese company means that the employee ________.
   A. leaves his company only when business is bad
   B. gets a job soon after he leaves school or university

C. can work there throughout his career

D. can have his serious mistakes in work corrected

2. Which of the following statements is INCORRECT?

A. Family and company interests are equally important.

B. The Japanese worker is very loyal to his company.

C. One's future is guaranteed through hard work.

D. Devotion to one's company is encouraged.

3. Lifetime employment influences one's ________.

A. achievements at work

B. performance at work

C. career options

D. attitude toward work

4. The Japanese worker is fond of his company's products because of ________.

A. his marriage with the daughter of the president

B. the close link between him and his company

C. his willingness to work overtime

D. his active participation in quality control

5. The passage mainly discusses ________.

A. how lifetime employment works in Japan

B. what benefits lifetime employment has brought to Japanese workers

C. what lifetime employment is

D. how lifetime employment is viewed

Cover Letters

The cover letter that one submits with a resumé can be as important as the resumé itself. Read the explanations of what to include in a cover letter and then write your own letter.

Street Address
City, State, Zip
Date

Name, Title
Company Name
Street Address
City, State, Zip

Dear ________________,

Paragraph 1. *Attract attention*. State who you are, why you are writing, and how you heard of the opening or the employer. Reference should be made to your specific interest in this organization and position.

Paragraph 2 & 3. *Arouse interest.* Here you can "editorialize", and amplify your unique qualifications and accomplishments. Do not simply restate information from your resumé, but rather draw conclusions, summarize, and indicate how your experiences and skills can be utilized in this organization and position.

Paragraph 4. *Indicate action.* State what action you will take (e.g., a follow-up phone call or letter) and when. The employer may wish to contact you first. Make this easy for the employer by providing current telephone numbers and area codes, and changes in address. Indicate when you will be available for an interview. State that you are enclosing a copy of your resumé.

Sincerely yours,

Signature

Typed Name

UNIT 11 Intercultural Negotiation

Pre-class Activity

Receiving Negotiation Groups

Suppose that your company is going to receive two negotiation groups. One is from America, and the other is from Japan. Both of them will stay in your city for 5 days. Now, draw up a reception agenda for the two groups respectively. And explain why you arrange their visit in that way.

Read to Learn More

Text

Negotiation Styles

Visit the business section of any Barnes & Noble or Borders bookstore and you will find numerous texts on negotiations. Using "negotiation" to search on Amazon.com will bring up more than 3,000 selections. Narrow the search by using "international negotiation" and you will still find over 1,000 entries. This is an easy way to discover the critical role that negotiation plays in international business. The process is so important that some estimates suggest international executives spend more than 20 percent of their time in negotiation activities. This is probably very conservative estimate, considering that negotiations are integral to all international mergers, joint ventures, import of raw materials, export of finished products, patent licensing agreements, and every other cross-cultural, commercial undertaking.

Both domestic and international business negotiations involve representatives from different organizations working to achieve mutually agreeable solutions, while concurrently trying to minimize differences, misunderstandings, and conflicts. To obtain these objectives, they rely on communication. The role of communication is so important that Drake calls it the "life-blood of negotiation" and considers it an area often overlooked in intercultural negotiation studies.

As you might suspect, culture plays a critical role when representatives from different nations set out to try to reach an accord acceptable to both sides. Marked by the participants' varying cultural values, ideals, beliefs, and behaviors, international negotiations offer a rich medium for misunderstanding and friction. So demanding is the task, one experienced negotiator has characterized "cross-cultural and international settings as the most challenging". This challenge arises because cross-cultural negotiation participants are influenced by their respective national bargaining style, which is often a product of contracting historical legacies, different cultural values, dissimilar decision-making processes, and varying attitudes toward conflict. During negotiations, these differences can exacerbate, and often obscure, the actual commercial issues under consideration.

To best demonstrate culture's influence on international business bargaining, we will examine three aspects related to the negotiation process: (1) participant perspective, (2) external factors, and (3) expected outcomes.

Participant Perspective. Culture will affect how people view the negotiation process as a whole, their perception of their counterparts, and how they actually conduct the bargaining sessions. For example, the U.S. approach to negotiations is a product of the classical Greek tradition of rhetorical eloquence, argumentation, debate, and persuasion. Drawing on this Aristotelian legacy, U.S. trade and corporate representatives frequently enter into negotiations with a direct, somewhat confrontational approach. They commonly view the bargaining process as adversarial in nature, driven by the underlying objective of wining. There is also an emphasis on quick results that maximize profits and produce a short-term perspective. Relationships with the other side, especially long-term relations, are a secondary consideration, if considered at all.

The U.S. outlook can easily create problems when negotiating with collective-based cultures. For example, Japanese and Chinese negotiators take a long-term view toward business ventures. Their first goal is to work on building a relationship, establishing a level of trust, and determining the desirability of entering into an extended association with the other organization. The approach is more collegial and the focus is on mutual interests, giving rise to a "win-win" perspective, which is quite in contrast to the more aggressive U.S. view of "business is business". For the Russians, negotiations are simply a forum for debate, an opportunity to convince the other side of the rightfulness of their position. The Russians often interpret an offer to make concessions as an indication of weakness. Rather than compromise on an issue, they will simply reiterate their original arguments in the expectation that the other negotiating team will ultimately realize the correctness of the Russian position.

The age of the negotiators can also be a factor. The Chinese have great respect for their elders and consider them to have more wisdom than younger people. But in Western societies, especially the U.S., age is less an issue than expertise or competency. A team of bright, young U.S. engineers sent to negotiate the specifics of a technology transfer project with a Chinese corporation may well encounter difficulties just because of their youthfulness. The Chinese negotiators, typically around fifty years of age, may have trouble seeing the U.S. team as credible or competent. The gender of the team members can also play a role in negotiations, especially in Muslim countries. In Saudi Arabia, where women are considered subordinate to men and are subject to many culturally based social restrictions, Saudi negotiators may have difficulty interacting with a female negotiator. The issue is so sensitive that some experts advise against including women on the negotiating team when dealing with Saudis.

External Factors. All negotiators hold culturally based expectations of how the bargaining process should proceed and what might be considered appropriate and inappropriate behaviors. This involves concepts such as the application of formality and informality, status of the members, view of time, role of government, ethical standards, display of emotions, and communication style.

As indicated, cultural values of formality and informality can influence people's dress, actions, and communication style. This becomes a particularly important aspect at the negotiation table. Negotiators from the U.S., a highly informal culture, tend to avoid titles and are quick to use first names soon after meeting someone. These actions can be quite disconcerting in European cultures, such as France, Germany, and England, where formality plays a greater role and titles are an important part of an individual's identity. Representatives from China, Japan, and Korea will also expect negotiations to be conducted on a more formal level than someone from Australia, an informal culture. Koreans prefer titles to names, even among themselves, according to Lewis.

The social or organizational status of members of the negotiating teams is another important cultural consideration. The U.S., being strongly egalitarian, is prone to select members based on their proven managerial or technical abilities, with little concern for their position. In other cultures, however, the status of team members is of considerable importance. The inclusion of high-ranking company officers or individuals form influential families is often an indication that the company is serious about negotiations, and wants to reach a successful agreement. In East Asia, the number of people assigned to the team will also signal the level of importance attached to the negotiations—the more participants, the greater the importance.

In the past, before becoming more culturally astute, U.S. businessmen were noted for arriving in Tokyo on Monday with hotel reservations booked for a one-week stay. Their plan was to begin negotiations on Tuesday and sign a contract by Friday so they could return home for the weekend.

These expectations often doomed the business transaction before the parties even met. The U.S. participants were enculturated to view time as a fixed commodity—something that should not be wasted. Thus, they were impatient to quickly move from one objective to the next, with a minimum of inactivity between each event. This Western desire to move the negotiations along rapidly is no popular approach in Japan and China. There is even an Asian proverb that states, "Patience is power; with time and patience the mulberry leaf becomes a silk gown." For these cultures time is perceived quite differently than in the West. In business, their first goal is to get to know the other party. The Japanese and the Chinese see entering into a commercial arrangement much like entering into a marriage. It is something that should last for a long time and be beneficial to both parties. Accordingly, they want to take time to ensure that relation with the other organization will be spent in entertainment and sightseeing activities in order to increase their knowledge of the members of the other negotiating team. Early meetings will focus more on the general background of the other organization and less on the specifics of the proposed business transaction.

The role that a nation's government plays in business is yet another factor in international negotiations. U.S. corporate negotiators consider government as separate and apart from the business transaction. The function of government is to establish and enforce laws designed to create a level playing field for economic activities. Active governmental involvement in commercial negotiations is seen as a potential obstruction to a successful conclusion between the involved parties.

Culture also shapes one's ethics, on both a personal and national level. As discussed earlier, in commercial dealings the U.S. has instituted law prohibiting the payment of bribes or giving of gifts that exceed $ 180. However, in some countries, payments or gifts used to "grease the wheels" are considered a natural part of doing business and permeates all levels of society. Dissimilar opinions on the appropriateness of providing payment to facilitate an international business arrangement can easily result in failed negotiations.

Emotional displays by negotiators can also have a bearing on the outcome of an international business transaction. For example, Western business representatives often characterize their Asian counterparts as "inscrutable" due to a lack of facial expressions displayed at the bargaining table. In the U.S., it is normal and expected for people to use a wide range of nonverbal behaviors as outward signs of their feelings. The U.S. culture teaches that it is a natural part of social interactions to signal pleasure, disgust, anger, or any other emotion through nonverbal displays. In China, Japan, and Korea, however, outward demonstrations of emotions are felt to disturb the harmony and are studiously avoided. Thus, at a negotiation table a Korean representative would consider a frowning U.S. counterpart to be rather immature. In other cultures, such as Mexico and those in the Middle East, expressed emotions are expected and seen as a means of emphasizing and reinforcing one's negotiation position. Beamer and Varner explain the role of emotion for a Kuwaiti negotiator, and the potential for an adverse reaction in this way:

His love of verbal play and the importance of emotion in communication may make the Kuwaiti negotiator's wording of messages seem theatrical to a low-context communicator [*e.g.*, *U.S. or Canadian*] *who shuns ambiguity and strives for directness and simplicity.*

A negotiator's communication style can also be the source of difficulties in international business. Representatives from collective cultures such as China, Japan, Korea, and Indonesia place considerable value on maintaining positive relations with their negotiation counterparts. To accomplish this, they rely on an indirect communication style. Sensitive issues with the potential to create conflict or cause discord are handled with care and normally addressed in an indirect manner. The Chinese and Japanese are reluctant to give a direct negative reply, relying instead on equivocal statements such as "that may be difficult," "we need to study that more," or "we are still thinking about it." The Indonesians are so concerned with maintaining harmonious relations they have "twelve ways to say 'no'". Indirectness of this magnitude can be the source of consternation, confusion, and even misinterpretation to the Western negotiator, who is used to "getting to the point" and "not beating around the bush". For example, if a Japanese negotiator tells his U.S. counterpart that a request "will be difficult", he is actually saying no and there will be no further consideration of the issue. However, the U.S. business representative is likely to interpret the statement as an indication that the request will remain under consideration, with a possible reply at a later date. Waiting for a response that will not come can quickly lead to strained relations.

Expected Outcomes. As with every other aspect of negotiations, culture also stills participants with an expectation as to what the bargaining should achieve, what form the end result should take. The varying cultural perceptions of business contracts were discussed earlier in this chapter, but the importance of these issues is worth reviewing from the context of negotiations. Coming from a highly legalistic society, U.S. negotiators see the final objective of successful negotiations as a signed and binding contract. The amount of importance that U.S. negotiators attach to contracts is best described by Salacuse:

> *For them* [*U.S.*] *the contract is a definitive set of rights and duties that strictly binds the two sides, controls their behavior in the future, and determines who does what, when and how. According to this view, the parties' deal is their contract.*

These expectations give rise to lengthy, detailed contracts, frequently involving lawyers or legal experts as part of the negotiating team. This perception is quite in contrast to collectivistic cultures, where business negotiations are considered a means of establishing long-term relationships rather than producing a legal document restricted to governing a single, specific transaction. From the Chinese perspective, the negotiations are designed to establish the parameters of the relationship, and the contract should serve only as an outline or a guide. Like the Chinese, the Japanese and the Saudis also dislike detailed contracts. The Japanese believe that since future events cannot be predicted, a contract must be flexible in order to accommodate situational and organizational changes.

(Adapted from Samovar, L. A., R. E. Porter, & E. R. McDaniel. 2009. *Communication Between Cultures*. 6th ed. Beijing: Peking University Press, pp. 245-249.)

After reading activity

1. What are the common factors in the U.S. negotiation style mentioned in the text? How could these factors cause problems while negotiating with Chinese counterparts?
2. When Japanese negotiator said: "that's difficult", it possibly posted cultural barrier for Americans to understand its true meaning. Could you list some other words or expressions in your language often used in negotiation process but may cause communication problems to Americans?
3. Why should factors as religion and gender also be considered in preparing cross-cultural negotiation process? Illustrate their influence with examples.

Kaleidoscope

Negotiation Styles of Different Cultures

Element	U.S. Americans	Japanese	Arabians	Mexicans
Group Composition	Marketing oriented	Function Oriented	Committee of specialists	Friendship oriented
Number involved	2-3	4-7	4-6	2-3
Space orientation	Confrontational; Competitive	Display harmonious relationship	Status	Close, friendly
Establishing rapport	Short period; direct to task	Longer period; until harmony	Longer period; until trusted	Longer period; discuss family
Exchange of information	Documented; step-by-step; multimedia	Extensive; Concentrate on receiving side	Less emphasis on technology, more on relationship	Less emphasis on technology, more on relationship
Persuasion tools	Time pressure; loss of saving/making money	Maintain relationship references; intergroup connections	Go-between hospitality	Emphasis on family and on social concerns; goodwill measured in generations
Use of language	Open/direct; sense of urgency	Indirect; appreciative; cooperative	Flattery; emotional; religious	Respectful; graciousness
First offer	Fair ±5% to 10%	±10% to 20%	±20% to 50%	Fair
Second offer	All to package; Sweeten the deal	-5%	-10%	Add incentive
Final offer	Total package	Make no further concessions	-25%	Total package

Continued

Element	U.S. Americans	Japanese	Arabians	Mexicans
Decision-making process	Top management team	Collective	Team makes recommendation	Senior manager and secretary
Decision maker	Top management team	Middle line with team consensus	Senior manager	Senior manager
Risk taking	Calculated; personal responsibility	Low group responsibility	Religion based	Personally responsible

(Adapted from 钱尼,马丁. 2013. 跨文化商务沟通(英文版)[M]. 6 版. 北京:中国人民大学出版社, p. 247.)

Mini-case Study

Cross-Cultural Negotiation

Martinez Construction is a well-established construction company in eastern Spain. A recent decline in contracts has revealed the need of expansion of the company into international market from local market. After some research and discussion, Diego Martinez, president and son of the founder of Martinez Construction, has come to the conclusion that the best approach will be through the acquisition of an existing company from the Thruhandanstalt (THA), a German company. Diego chose his brother-in-law and manager of the Barcelona branch of Martinez Construction, Juan Sanchez, to act as the negotiator for the company with the THA. Juan will be accompanied by Diego's nephew and project manager of the new German acquisition, Miguel Martinez.

At the time of arrival in Germany, Juan felt that he was having a difficult time just getting acquainted with the Germans. He felt pressured by the THA representatives. The Germans were all business; they didn't seem to have time to get to know Juan personally: rush and urgency to complete the sale was scheduled for 9:00 A.M. Juan and MKiguel arrived at 9:15. Juan noticed that the THA representative, Helga Schmidt, seemed quite agitated when they arrived. She didn't even offer them coffee. He wondered what had upset her so much.

When he suggested that they be taken on a tour of the city this morning instead of immediately starting the negotiations, he was reminded of the necessity of proceeding with the negotiations. Even though this displeased Juan, he agreed to start negotiations for the sale.

The Germans presented their proposal to Juan. He was amazed. Every detail was in this contract; and yet the THA had not yet ascertained the financial status and position of the construction firm in Leipzig. For this reason, Juan had expected some sort of flexible agreement. This was especially important since there was no way to determine the extent of future problems given the dearth of available financial analysis. Didn't the Germans know this? If the THA was to be trusted, why bother with this type of contract? He told the Germans exactly what his thoughts were on this subject.

Helga was clearly uncomfortable with Juan's emotional outburst. However, she did see his point and decided to compromise by offering a phased contract, which made Juan more comfortable with the situation. However, the Germans felt lost without the technicalities represented in the original contract.

The negotiations proceeded smoothly from this point. The final contract stated that in two years they would review the original price and recalculate it based on new and presumably more reliable data concerning the true value of the firm. Although there were problems with the negotiations, one thing did impress Juan about the Germans. He really appreciated the way the negotiations were organized. When there was a question, Helga always knew whom to contact. She also knew what forms, reports, and so on, needed to be sent to which department of the THA. Helga, on the other hand, was very uncomfortable with Juan's relaxed manner. However, she did value his genuineness and practicality.

(Source: Deresky, H. 2002. *International Management*, 4th Ed. New Jersey: Prentice Hall.)

Questions

1. How do you see the members of Juan's negotiation team? What are reasons for Juan to choose them? Do you think his team will work effectively in the negotiation?
2. Why did Juan feel getting acquainted with the Germans so important for him? And in what way did he try to gain a chance to get acquainted with them?
3. How are Juan and Helga different in the manner of dealing with time?
4. Why was Juan unsatisfied with the first offer given by the Germans? What did a contract mean to each side?
5. Why did Helga feel uncomfortable with Juan's emotional outburst? How do Germans manage emotions traditionally?
6. What things left deep impressions on Juan? And why did he feel that way?
7. What kinds of culture does each negotiation party represent for?

After-class Exercises

Reading

Differences in culture between deal makers can obstruct negotiations in many ways. First, they can create misunderstandings in communication. If one American executive responds to another American's proposal by saying, "that's difficult," the response, interpreted against American culture and business practice, probably means that the door is still open for further discussion, that perhaps the other side should sweeten its offer. In some other cultures, for example in Asia, persons may be reluctant to say a direct and emphatic "no", even when that is their intent. So when a Japanese negotiator, in response to a proposal says, "that is difficult," he is clearly indicating that the proposal is unacceptable. "It is difficult" means "no" to the Japanese, but to the American it means "maybe".

Second, cultural differences create difficulties not only in understanding words, but also in interpreting actions. For example, most Westerners expect a prompt answer when they make a statement or ask a question. Japanese, on the other hand, tend to take longer to respond. As a result, negotiations with Japanese are sometimes punctuated with periods of silence that seem excruciating to an American. For the Japanese, the period of silence is normal, an appropriate time to reflect on what has been said. The fact that they may not be speaking in their native language lengthens even more the time needed to respond.

From their own cultural perspective, Americans may interpret the Japanese silence as rudeness, lack of understanding, or a cunning tactic to get the Americans to reveal themselves. Rather than wait for a response, the American tendency is to fill the void with words by asking questions, offering further explanations, or merely repeating what they have already said. This response to silence may confuse the Japanese, who are made to feel that they are being bombarded by questions and proposals without being given adequate time to respond to any of them.

On the other hand, Latin Americans, who place a high value on verbal agility, have a tendency to respond quickly. Indeed, they may answer a point once they have understood it even though the other side has not finished speaking. While inexperienced American negotiators are sometimes confused by Japanese delays in responding, they can become equally agitated in negotiations with Brazilians by what Americans consider constant interruptions.

Third, cultural considerations also influence the form and substance of the deal you are trying to make. For example, in many parts of the Moslem world, where Islamic law prohibits the taking of interest on loans, one may need to restructure or relabel finance charges in a deal as "administrative fees" in order to gain acceptance at the negotiation table. More substantively, differences in culture will invariably require changes in products, management systems, and personnel practices. For example, in Thailand, the relationship between manager and employee is more hierarchical than it is in the United States. Workers are motivated by a desire to please the manager, but they in turn expect and want their managers to sense their personal problems and be ready to help with them. In other cultures, for example in Australia, employees neither expect nor want managers to become involved with employees' personal problems. Thus an Australian project in Thailand would need to change its concept of employee relations because of the local culture.

Questions

1. What is the possible real intention for Asians to say "it's difficult"?

2. What does a long pause or silence during a talk mean to Americans and Japanese respectively?
3. How should you deal with the frequent interruption from your Latin counterparts in the middle of conversation?
4. Aside from communication styles, what others cultural factors may influence the negotiation process?
5. A Chinese negotiation team received an invitation from their Greek counterparts, inviting them to attend a dinner at 12 o'clock. The Chinese negotiators arrived at the written location at noon, but no one showed up. They waited for another half of an hour, but still, nothing happened. They looked at the invitation again and again, but the place and the time were all clear and right. Could you tell what the problem is?
6. One French businessman who just made a big deal with a Chinese private-owned company complained to Wu Jianming, the former China to France ambassador: "I don't want to make business with that man (the owner of the Chinese company) again!" Wu didn't understand why he said that since he just signed three contacts with him. The Frenchman explained: "This man was looking around all the time during our talking. It seemed that he did not want to look at me at all. This is a big humiliation to me." How could you explain the Chinese businessman's behavior? What other etiquettes should we follow in an international negotiation?

UNIT 12 Building a Team with Intercultural Competence

Pre-class Activity

Americans in Your Eyes

What is your understanding of Americans? Please write down your answers.

1. Americans are...
2. Americans women/men are...
3. Americans like to do...
4. American students are...
5. American education system is...
6. American society is...
7. American foreign policy is...

......

You may write more about the United States of America you know and exchange your notes with your classmates to see the differences and common points. Then try to classify your answers into two groups and fill out the following table.

Facts	Stereotypes

Finally, with the knowledge you have acquired now, do you think you can fit in the life in America without too much trouble? If there are problems, what are they supposed to be?

Read to Learn More

Text

The Need for Intercultural Business Communication Competence

By Linda Beamer and Iris Varner

What does culture have to do with business? Many business majors and practitioners immersed in questions of financial forecasting, market studies, and management models have turned aside from the question of culture and how it affects business. Unlike the hard data from measurable issues, culture is soft and slippery; you can't really grasp culture in your two hands and understand what you've got.

But more and more organizations are finding themselves involved in communication across cultures, between cultures, among cultures—because they are doing business in foreign countries, perhaps, or because they are sourcing from diverse backgrounds and different languages are working side by side in many countries. Intercultural communication at work is not the goal of some distant future; it is a real need here and now.

At its lowest level, business communication with unfamiliar cultures means simply finding a translator for conducting discussions in a foreign language. However, as more and more corporations are finding out, communication is about meanings, but not just words.

In order to understand the significance of a message from someone, you need to understand the way that person looks at the world, and the values that weigh heavy in that person's cultural backpack. You need to understand the meanings that are not put into words, the importance of the words that are used, and the way the message is organized and transmitted. You also need to know what to expect when that other person engages in a particular communication behaviors such as making a decision known, or negotiating a sales agreement, or writing a legal document such as a contract. And it would be wise of you to know something about the organization that person works in and how its structure affects communication.

Intercultural Business Communication Competence and Growing Domestic Diversity

All over the world nations are trying to come to terms with the growing diversity of their populations. Reactions range from acceptance to mere tolerance to rejection. As migrations of workers and refugees have increased globally, some countries are trying to control diversity by establishing strict guidelines for immigration from other countries. Other countries are attempting to develop government policies concerning the rights of immigrants to preserve their own cultures in adopted homelands. Canada is an example of a country where federal and provincial governments have Ministers of Multiculturalism to protect the cultural "mosaic" pattern that immigrants bring to

Canada.

The United States historically offered a home to more people of diverse cultures than any other country. But even in the United States, with its ideals of equality and tolerance, the advantages and disadvantages of acknowledging diversity are hotly debated. Recently some social critics in the United States have voiced oppositions to measures that preserve immigrant's cultural differences. They say the insistence on diversity actually separates Americans from one another by forcing them to focus on what differentiates them. Some authors argue that the "melting pot" that describes American culture depends upon the fusing of all other cultural identities into one. They claim that efforts to preserve immigrant cultures actually divide immigrants into categories, instead of treating them all as one "American" group. They suggest this is contrary to the American ideal of offering equal Americanness to everybody. Furthermore, they warn that multiculturalism may threaten the very characteristic that is so American: the union of one from many.

Today in the United States, a longstanding tradition of tolerance coexists side by side with an aversion to difference. Uniformity (for people of all countries) is easier to deal with than diversity. Diversity is difficult. Often the impulse to deny cultural differences comes from an embarrassment at focusing on difference, since frequently to be different in the United States is to be excluded. It isn't polite to point out that someone looks different, talks differently, wears different clothes, or eats different food. So, many times out of concern to avoid making someone feel uncomfortable, difference is played down.

This attitude may be motivated by a sincere desire for equal behavior toward people, regardless of their ethnic or cultural background, under the all-encompassing umbrella of ideal of equality. After all, most people who call themselves "American" have ancestors who were immigrants. Today many still have a strong desire to include newcomers in a friendly and tolerant national embrace and to affirm the high priority of equality in American culture.

But the truth is that people from different cultures really are different. That's a great strength of the human race and potential source of delight and wonderment as much as of fear and suspicion—the choice is ours. People of different cultures begin with different databases; we use different operating environments; we run different software and process information differently—we may even have different goals. To pretend we're all alike underneath is wrong and can lead to ineffectual communication, or worse.

While the debate is growing about how much to focus on cultural diversity, in fact cultural diversity is the reality. Businesses must deal with it. Individuals within organizations must also come to terms with diversity. The way to deal with diversity is not to deny it or ignore it, but to learn about differences so they don't impair communication or business transactions.

The description of the United States as a "meltpot", they created a new culture with distinct differences based on cultural heritage. As the new immigrants arrive, the United States culture becomes a "spicy stew". The potatoes stay potatoes, the carrots stay carrots, the onions stay onions, but all take on certain characteristics of each others' flavors. This blending creates a unique combination that gains from each ingredient. The United States' value of tolerance allows immigrants the freedom to keep their own identities while becoming part of a new culture. It is an ideal, but it is also achievable; in fact, it already exists to a degree in some communities in the United States.

Cultural differences don't prevent us from working with each other or communicating with each other or having productive business transactions. Indeed, we must learn to work with each other. The future of any organization depends on it. The reality is that businesses will increasingly be spicy stews of cultures, and so increasingly will the whole globe they inhabit. This fact is one reason why we must all acknowledge diversity and accept it. Another reason is that immigrants can add enormously to the society's—or an organization's—culture.

The biggest gain from accepting cultural differences is that cultural diversity enriches each one of us. People around the world and throughout history have developed a stunning variety of social systems and hierarchies of values. As a member of the human race, you can claim your rightful part—ownership of this richness, and you can celebrate the fertility of the human imagination along with its diverse products.

The essential ingredient for a successful cultural stew is skill in intercultural communication. Companies like Hewlett-Packard in the United States have discovered the value of intercultural communication skill and the increased productivity they bring about, and they have instituted diversity programs to train employees. They understand that the first step in effective intercultural communication is acceptance of diversity. This means we examine our own values for business, determine where the differences lie, and see how we can best overcome the differences and work together.

The Foundation for Intercultural Business Communication

The first step in effective intercultural communication is the understanding and acceptance of differences. That does not mean we have to agree with another culture's viewpoint, or that we have to adopt another culture's values. It does mean we and they examine our and their priorities and determine how we all can best work together, while being different.

In the process, we will realize that a person entering another culture will always have to adapt to a number of cultural conditions. That doesn't mean turning one's back on one's own culture or denying its priorities. Rather, it means learning what motivates others and how other cultural priorities inform the behavior, attitudes and values of business colleagues. This approach means adding to one's own culture, not subtracting from it. For example, a businessperson from New Zealand going to Japan must adapt to many Japanese practices, just as a Japanese businessperson going to New Zealand must adapt to a variety of New Zealand practices.

In attempting to understand another culture's perspective, we will be further ahead if we take off our own cultural blinders and develop sensitivity in the way we speak and behave. That is not always easy. We are all culturally based and culturally biased.

(Adapted from 庄恩平. 2011. 跨文化商务沟通[M]. 北京:首都经济贸易大学出版社,pp. 278-282.)

After reading activity

1. ***Rewrite the following sentences in your own words.***

1) Culture is soft and slippery.

2) Canada is an example of a country where federal and provincial governments have Ministers of Multiculturalism to protect the cultural "mosaic" pattern that immigrants bring to Canada.

3) But the truth is that people from different cultures really are different. That's a great strength of the human race and potential source of delight and wonderment as much as of fear and suspicion—the choice is ours.

4) As a member of the human race, you can claim your rightful part-ownership of this richness, and you can celebrate the fertility of the human imagination along with its diverse products.

5) In attempting to understand another culture's perspective, we will be further ahead if we take off our own cultural blinders and develop sensitivity in the way we speak and behave.

2. ***In the text, the author used figurative languages to create vivid images of different types of cultural patterns. Can you point them out? Which way of saying can indicate the cultural pattern in your country?***

Kaleidoscope

(1)

Defining Intercultural Competence

Most of the research in the area of communication competence maintains that in selecting the most appropriate course of action (exercising free choice), effective communicators are those who are (1) motivated, (2) have a fund of knowledge to draw upon, (3) possess requisite communication skills, and (4) are of good character. Let us look at these four components as a general prologue to a detailed analysis of intercultural competence.

Motivation. Motivation as it relates to competence means that as a communicator you want to interact with someone from another culture. If you allow feelings of anxiety, ethnocentrism and prejudice to control your actions, you will obviously lack the motivation necessary to be an effective communicator. Instead, you need to be committed to the entire communication process.

Knowledge. The knowledge dimension of communication competence means that you have a fund of knowledge about the other person and their culture. Luckmann points out the need for knowledge as it applies to the health care profession: "Nurses who are not knowledgeable about cultural differences risk misinterpreting patients' attempts to communicate. As a result, patients may not receive the proper care." According to Morreale, Spitzberg, and Barge, you need two kinds of knowledge to be competent—content knowledge and procedural knowledge. "Content knowledge involves knowing what topics, words, meanings, and so forth are required in a situation. Procedural knowledge is knowing how to assemble, plan and perform content knowledge in a particular situation." You need this knowledge so you can get to know what communication strategies to employ, what is proper protocol, and what customs need to be observed.

Skills. Skills are the actual application of specific behaviors that enable you to accomplish your goals. This point is further explained by Morreale, Spitzberg, and Barge when they observe, "skills are goal-directed because they must be designed to accomplish something." According to Smith and Bond, the skills need to be adapted to the rules of interaction that are appropriate to the host culture. You have learned those skills all your life so you can function effectively as a member of your culture. However, skills that are successful with one group, such as maintaining direct eye contact to show interest, may be inappropriate in cultures such as the Japanese, which finds such eye contact too obtrusive.

Character. While most of the literature dealing with communication competency includes only the three components we have just mentioned, it is our belief that one more feature needs to be added to the profile of a competent communicator. This attribute is character. The idea behind including character is simple—if you are not perceived by your communication partner as a person of good character your chances for success will be diminished. In many ways your character is composed of both your personal history and how you exhibit that history. As the American philosopher and teacher P. B. Fitzwater noted, "character is the sum and total of a person's choice." The key, of course, is how you act out those choices when you interact with someone from another culture. Perhaps the single most important trait associated with people of character is their trustworthiness. Characteristics often associated with the trustworthy person are integrity, honor, altruism, sincerity, and good will.

(Adapted from Samovar, L. A., R. E. Porter, & E. R. McDaniel. 2009. *Communication Between Cultures*. 6th ed. Beijing: Peking University Press, pp. 314-316.)

(2)

List of Intercultural Competence

This is a list for you to self-test your intercultural competence in the three dimensions of Motivation, Knowledge and Skills.

Knowledge:

1. I know the concept of culture and some cultural patterns (e.g., individualism / collectivism, high-context / low-context, etc.).
2. I know the social norms of my culture and consider my values and behaviours in accordance with the mainstream values.
3. I have acquired some knowledge about some important American geographical, historical, religions and socio-political factors (I have acquired some basic knowledge about some important geographical, historical, religions and socio-political factors of ××× countries).
4. I can contrast my own values and behaviours with those of ××× countries.
5. I recognize signs of culture stress and some strategies for overcoming it.

Motivation:

1. I am willing to show interest in cultural aspects (e.g., to understand the values, history, traditions, etc.) of ××× (people).
2. I am willing to try to understand differences in the behaviours, values, attitudes, and styles of ××× (people).
3. I am willing to adapt my behaviours to communicate appropriately with××× (people) (e.g., hugging) /×××(people) (e.g., hugging is acceptable between friends of the same sex but not between friends of different sexes).
4. I am willing to look for an alternative way to communicate with ××× (people) effectively (e.g., express my ideas clearly / not being too assertive).
5. I am willing to suspend judgment and appreciate the complexities of communicating and interacting interculturally.
6. I am willing to deal with the great uncertainty and anxiety in intercultural communication.

Skills:

1. I display respect to people from different cultures.
2. I use active listening skills while talking with people from other cultures.
3. I will use communication skills, such as explanation, clarification, and repetition to increase communication efficiency.
4. I use learning strategies, such as observation and reflection, to help me understand the cultural difference.
5. I adjust my behaviours to avoid offending people from different cultures.
6. I demonstrate flexibility when interacting with persons from different cultures.

Mini-case Study

From Embarrassment to Friendship

Shortly after we came to China, Bryan invited the heads of many Chinese publishing companies to a banquet to thank them for their support over the years. Since he was new to his post, Bryan had to toast each of the publishers individually to show his appreciation. In a display of sincerity, he emptied his glass with each of the toast. Pretty soon, the alcohol was getting to his head. He excused himself to use the bathroom, but as he got up, he stumbled on something and fell.

He was horrified. In the United States, it would be a sure loss of face. Much to his surprise, however, the Chinese publishers loved him for that. They had never met a foreigner who drank so much to befriend them. They found him trustworthy and down-to-earth. As a result, Bryan has had a great working relationship with these publishers. His little drunken accident had turned out to be a great blessing.

(Adapted from Ellis. Y. S. & B. D. Ellis. 2012. *101 Stories for Foreigners to Understand Chinese People*. Beijing: China Intercontinental Press.)

Questions

1. What did Bryan know about business protocols in China?
2. How did Bryan adjust his behaviors to cater for his Chinese counterparts?
3. How did Bryan win the trust of those Chinese publishers?
4. If the banquet was held in America and those publishers were Americans, how would Americans see this drunken accident? Would the working relationship be established successfully?
5. If you were Bryan, what would you think of your new working position in China?

After-class Exercises

Reading

Become a Culturally Competent Expat

By Michael Gates

Wal-Mart recently announced it was pulling out of Germany, losing $1 billion along the way. Critics said it failed to understand the culture.

Its attempt to introduce "greeters" to every store, with orders to smile at every customer, is said to have been particularly unpopular.

As we become more global the skill of seeing things from other cultures' points of view is becoming vital. Not just for the success of corporations but also for individuals to pursue careers and lead happy lives as expatriates.

People are moving to live and work abroad at record rates according to UN figures released in June. But while this may make logical career and business sense, human beings defy logic.

By the age of seven or so we have silently absorbed different values—or prioritised them differently—from other cultures. So while a toothy grin may create a positive climate for business in USA, in Germany it may be seen as a suspect intrusion of privacy.

The challenge is that we acquire our own culture so early we don't realize we have it. And our behaviour reflects this: all we do and say sends out unintended messages to our new colleagues, acquaintances and neighbours.

A personal defining moment was on moving to Finland nearly 20 years ago when a "how are you today?" was met with the stony "You asked me that last week".

We typically assume the worst and accuse the host culture of unfriendliness or irrationality. But we have to tease out the values beneath to know what is really going on.

In this Finnish case, privacy ("Why should I tell you how I am if I hardly know you?") and honesty ("If I say 'fine, thanks' and I am not, then I am lying.") are both involved.

We should also know our own values and where they may cause misunderstanding and loss of trust. Most of all we must realize that we are not normal. What is "normal" anyway? We must also appreciate why we are as we are.

This requires us to consider our attitudes to time, space, truth, individuality, authority, etc., and where they came from. Comparing how parents interact with children in the host and our own culture is not a bad place to start.

In USA children are generally taught to speak up for themselves and assert their individuality. Small wonder they develop into confident adults who believe "a fight is communication".

And what are the origins of culture? What in our climate, history, religion and language made our ancestors start thinking and behaving differently?

It's a fascinating voyage of discovery: like working out where your children's physical and mental traits have come from. The difference being that this is not genetic but cultural DNA—something we have learned and share with other members of our cultural group.

Interest in cross-cultural issues has been growing, as increasingly we come into contact with people different from us. There are now some great books to help us see ourselves as others see us.

But how can we cope with the inevitable cultural differences we will come across?

First, it's useful to get to grips with a general theory before trawling through lots of disparate trivia about different cultures. There are over 200 national cultures in the world, and we can't hope to know everything.

One useful theory is the Lewis Model of culture, behind the Culture Active program. Richard D. Lewis classifies cultures into three main types—linear-active, multi-active and reactive—described in detail in the book *When Cultures Collide*. Other well-known models are by the authors Geert Hofstede and Fons Trompenaars.

But the ultimate key has to be the ability to adapt how we communicate.

I was once on a Lufthansa flight where we suddenly experienced turbulence. The captain spoke first in German with an explanation of the cause; of the action he would take, and what he would do if this failed. He then gave relevant technical specifications. The Germans visibly relaxed.

There were also Brits and Americans on board. The captain changed into English and simply announced: "We're on a bit of a roller-coaster, so just belt yourselves tight, sit back, and enjoy the ride!" We smiled and breathed a collective sigh of relief.

That's what I call culturally-competent communication.

About the author:

Michael Gates was a scholar of St. Catherine's College Oxford, where he gained an M.A. in English Language and Literature. He worked for five years in radio before he helped establish the Finnish office of Richard Lewis Communications, who give cross-cultural, communication skills and business language training world-wide.

(Source: Gates, M. 2006. *Become a Culturally Competent Expat*. Retrieved from http://www.Telegraph.co.uk)

Questions

1. How did critics say about Wal-Mart's failure in Germany?
2. What policy was responsible for Wal-Mart's failure according to the article?
3. Why do Finnish people react coolly to a warm greeting: "How are you today?"
4. What cause one culture differing from another?
5. What would help you to understand cultural differences?
6. Why did the writer regard the German captain's explanation of the turbulence as a culturally-competent communication?

Group Project

Topic: A Study on the Adaptability of Foreigners at ××× University.

Instruction: Form a research group of 4-5 people. Interview foreigners living on your campus and find out how foreigners adapt to the life at your university. Three research domains are suggested: the adaptability of foreign environment, the adaptability of new education system, the adaptability of interpersonal relationship. After the data are collected, use intercultural theories to analyze and explain it.

参考文献

Althen, G. & J. Bennett. (2011). *American Ways: A Cultural Guide to the United States*. 3rd Edition. Boston/London: Intercultural Press.

Deresky, H.(2002). *International Management*. 4th Edition. New Jersey: Prentice Hall.

Ellis, Y. S., & B. D. Ellis. (2012). 101 *Stories for Foreigners to Understand Chinese People*. Beijing: China Intercontinental Press.

Hall, E. T. (1989). *Beyond Culture*. New York: Anchor books.

Hofstede, G. (2001). *Cultures Consequences: Comparing Values, Behavior, Institutions and Organizations Across Nations* , 2nd Edition. CA: Sage Publications.

Hofstede, G.(1984). "National cultures and corporate cultures". In L. A. Samovar & R. E. Porter (Eds.), *Communication Between Cultures*. Belmont, CA: Wadsworth.

Hu, W., et al. (2010). *Encountering the Chinese: A Modern Country, An Ancient Culture*. 3rd Edition. Boston/London: Intercultural Press.

Kluckhohn, C., & W. H. Kelly. (1945). "The concept of culture". In R. Linton (Ed.). *The Science of Man in the World Culture*. New York: Columbia University Press.

Kroeber, A. L., & C. Kluckhohn. (1952). *Culture: A Critical Review of Concepts and Definitions*. Harvard University Peabody Museum of American Archeology and Ethnology Papers.

Lederach, J. P. (1995). *Preparing for Peace: Conflict Transformation Across Cultures*. NY: Syracuse University Press.

Levine, D. R., & M. B. Adelman. (1993). *Beyond Language: Cross-cultural Communication*. 2nd Edition. New Jersey: Prentice Hall Regents.

Linell, D. (2001). *Doing Culture: Cross-Cultural Communication in Action*. Beijing: Foreign Language Teaching and Research Press.

Linton, R. (1945). *The Cultural Background of Personality*. New York: Greenwood-Heinemann Publishing.

Lustig, M. W. & J. Koester. (2010). *Intercultural Competence: Interpersonal Communication Across Cultures*. 6th Edition. Boston: Pearson.

Moran, P. R. (2002). *Teaching Culture: Perspectives in Practice*. Beijing: Foreign Language Teaching and Research Press.

Samovar, L. A., et al. (2009). *Communication Between Cultures*. 6th Edition. Beijing: Peking University Press.

Stella, T. (1999). *Communication Across Cultures*. New York/London: The Guilford Press.

窦卫霖. (2007). 跨文化商务交流案例分析[M]. 北京:对外经济贸易大学出版社.

钱尼,马丁. (2013). 跨文化商务沟通(英文版)[M]. 6 版. 北京:中国人民大学出版社.